Santa Barbara
All About the Red-Tile City

Santa Barbara

All About the Red-Tile City

Mary Zeldis
photos by Bill Zeldis

ZELDIS PUBLISHING
SANTA BARBARA, CALIFORNIA

ZELDIS PUBLISHING

Santa Barbara, California

©2004 by Mary Zeldis

All rights reserved. No photographs or text may be reproduced or utilized in any form, or by electronic, mechanical, or other means without the prior written permission of the publisher.

Library of Congress Cataloging-in-Publication Data

Zeldis, Mary, 06/05/48-.

Santa Barbara, All About the Red-Tile City / Mary Zeldis.

p.   cm.

ISBN 0-9719080-9-5

1. Santa Barbara   2. Local guidebook   I. Title.

Book Design / Lucy Brown Design

Photo Portraits / Leisbeth Lagendyk

Printed in Hong Kong

*I dedicate this book
to those who created
and maintain this beautiful city,
to my teachers,
and to Bill, the photographer
who brings excitement and color
to this book
and to my life.*

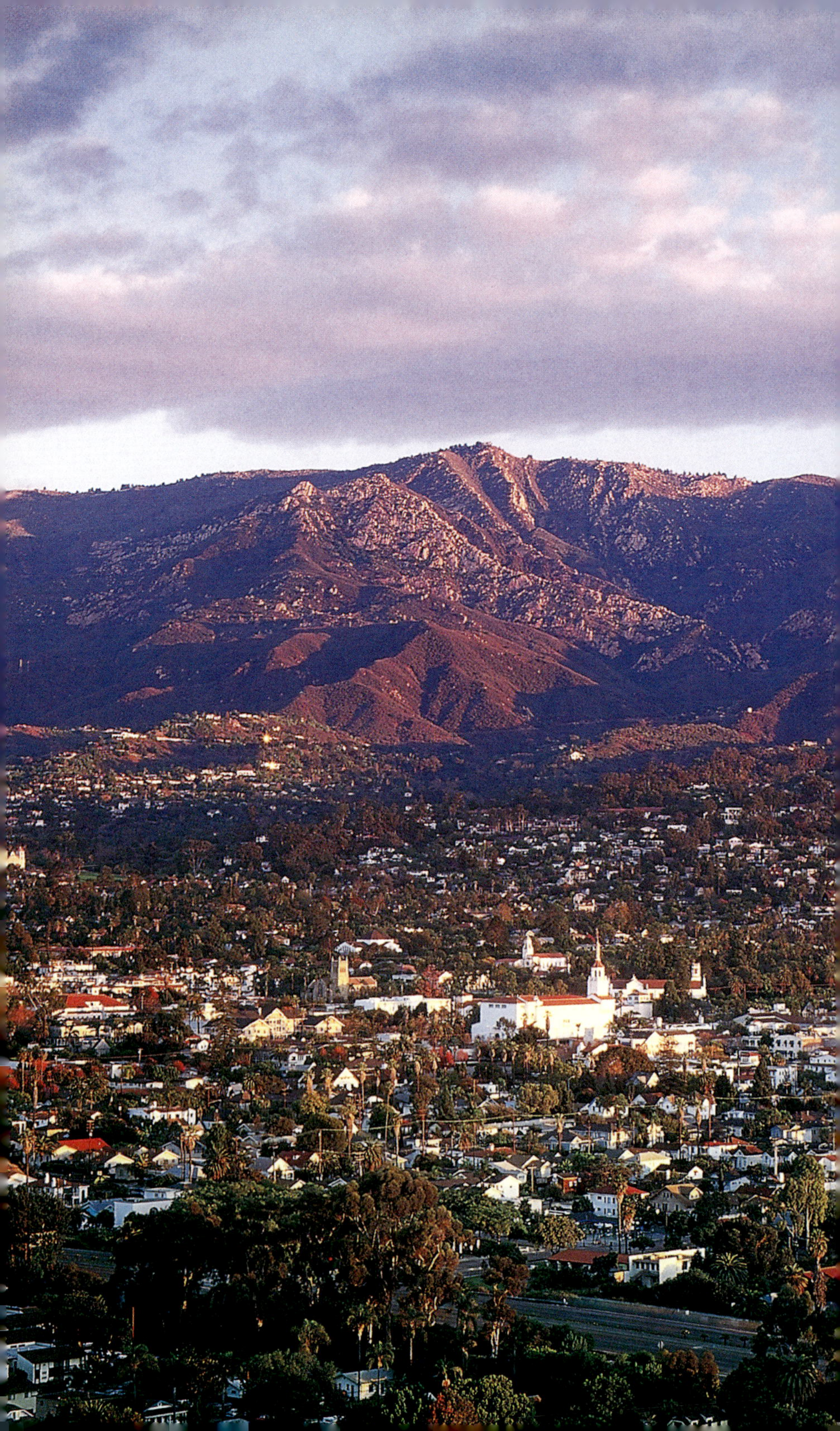

Contents

Acknowledgments   9

CHAPTER ONE
History
11

CHAPTER TWO
The Ocean and Beach
31

CHAPTER THREE
Art and Architecture
51

CHAPTER FOUR
Parks and Gardens
69

Best Places in Santa Barbara   86

Celebrations and Seasonal Events   93

ACKNOWLEDGMENTS

I wish to thank Carolyn Bond, my friend and editor; Lucy Brown for her imaginative design; Kirk Loggins for moral support and technical advice; Mary Louise Days at the Santa Barbara Trust for Historical Preservation, Michael Redmon at the Santa Barbara Historic Society, and Peggy Hayes at the Santa Barbara Courthouse for their generosity in providing historical background; Laurie Hannah at the Santa Barbara Botanic Garden, and Kathleen Sullivan at Santa Barbara City Parks, for their help with the chapter on parks and gardens; the Santa Barbara Public Library's resource desk; the Santa Barbara Adult Education program and its teachers Len Van Nostrand, Belma Johnson, and Paula Sandefur; friends and neighbors who helped with compiling the information on best places; the Santa Barbara Visitor Center; Eric Kelley for his advice and encouragement; Tom Hummel at Toppan Printing; and last but not least, my husband, Bill, for his photographs and support.

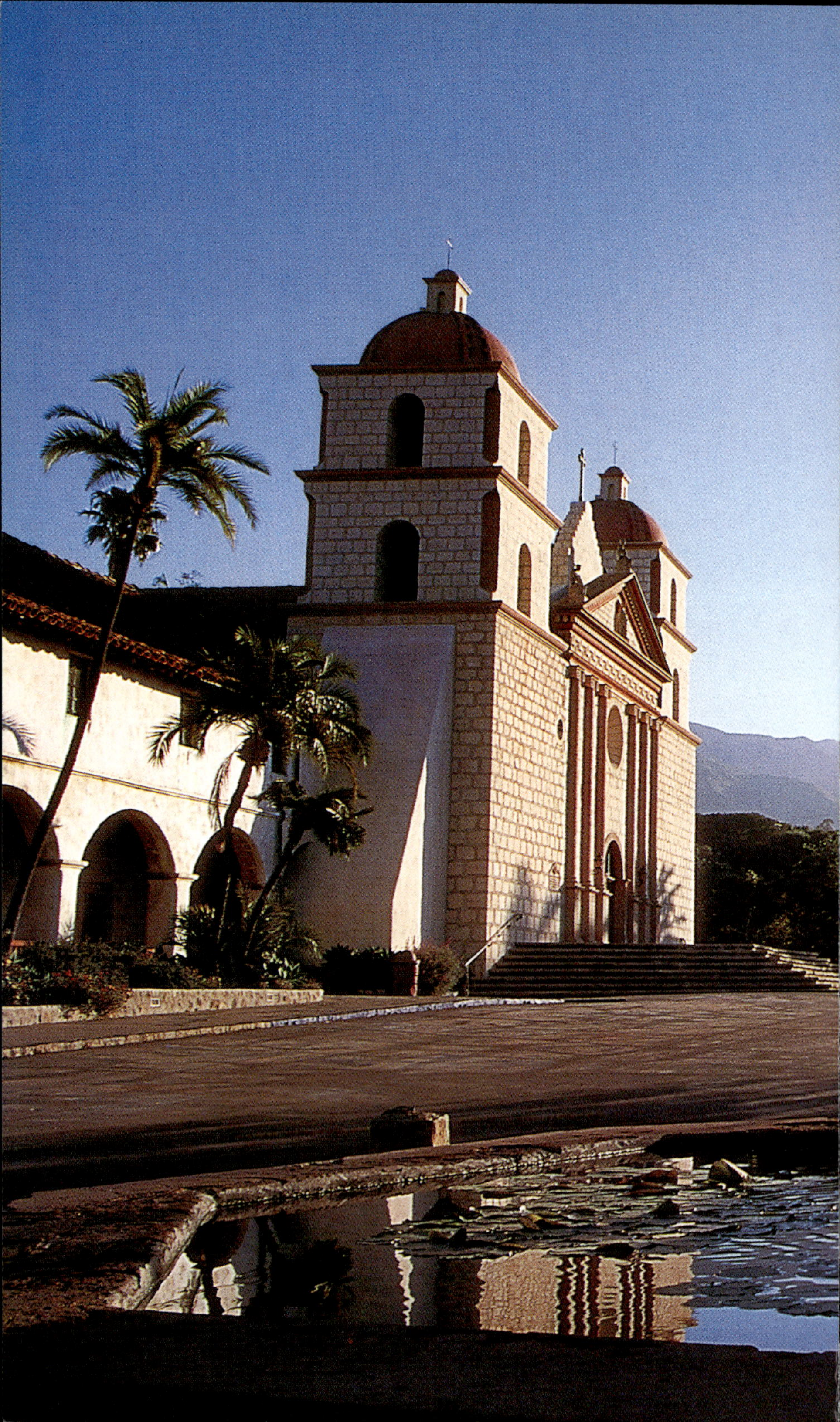

The History
CHAPTER ONE

By nature, Santa Barbara is a paradise. Situated on a rare section of California coastline that runs east/west, where the south-facing slopes of the coastal range meet the sea, Santa Barbara is protected from storms by both the mountains and the offshore islands. In this secluded garden constructed by nature herself, the average temperature varies only eight to ten degrees during the year.

Archeological evidence suggests that some of the first humans on the North American continent, more than 13,000 years ago, lived right here. And why not? The weather is nearly perfect—sunny most days, with just enough morning fog during the summer months for comfort. There are few storms yet enough gentle rain for some tropical, and many subtropical, plants and animals to thrive. The air is teeming with birds; 473 species have been counted here! The sea brims with fish and other marine

Santa Barbara Mission

life. Early written accounts by Europeans describe the Chumash Indians living here comfortably through all the seasons, needing no more shelter than their grass huts. Gazing upon this lush Eden, it is clear that long before the city of Santa Barbara was established, mother nature was smiling on this shore.

In 1542, Juan Rodriguez Cabrillo, in the service of Spain, sailed through what is now our city's harbor as he explored northward from Mexico, hoping to discover a body of water that linked the Atlantic and Pacific oceans. Sixty years later, Sebastian Vizcaino sailed up the coast from Mexico, charting the coastline and looking for a good harbor for the Spanish. On the eve of December 4, 1602, the feast day of St. Barbara, he sailed into our channel, so he named the place Santa Barbara.

In April of 1782, by command of the king of Spain, a group of overland explorers traveled north to Santa Barbara en route from Mexico to Monterey, where the Spanish had already established an outpost. The Russians, who had claimed land in Alaska, had begun to explore the California coast, and the Spanish, sensing competition, were anxious to expand Spanish influence and culture, and assert their presence. These explorers included Governor Neve, the governor of Spanish Alta California, and Lieutenant Jose Francisco Ortega and his men. When Father Junipero Serra, a Franciscan friar and Missionary President of Upper (Alta) California, heard of the Spanish king's proposal to establish a string of missions about a day's travel apart in Alta California, he decided to join the expedition. In the middle of April 1782, the travelers established the Buenaventura Mission (now in the city of Ventura), twenty-seven miles south of Santa Barbara. Their next step was to look for a site for a presidio to protect and defend the region between Monterey and San Diego.

About a week later, they arrived in the Santa Barbara region, where they found many thriving Indian villages with friendly inhabitants. The native Chumash Indians had a culture with peaceful ways, and sufficient food, clothing, and shelter were available in this gentle land to afford them the luxury of time to play and sing. They welcomed the European strangers with great hospitality. Indeed, the Indians were so friendly that they hampered the efforts of the Europeans intent on "discovering" a land the Chumash knew all about. Here is an entry from the diary of one such serious explorer: "Our only object in traveling today was to get rid of so many people…They were not satisfied with spreading food before us, but also desired to amuse us." Imagine! He complains further that even after his group thought they were rid of the Chumash's distracting congeniality, the same Indians returned at nightfall to make loud music, destroying the dutiful explorers' sleep! Evidently, hospitality and a big welcome for the visitor have a long history in this corner of the world.

Father Serra's heart's desire was to establish a mission among these welcoming Indians. But the governor had other plans; he told the padre to wait until the safety of the region was assured before erecting a mission church. His dream deferred, Father Serra did his priestly duty, consecrating the ground for the presidio, and then left, dejected, walking all the way to Monterey, even though he was seventy years old.

The Presidio and the Mission

The fledgling El Presidio de Santa Barbara was founded April 21, 1782, near a native village ruled by the amicable Chief Yanonalit. Simple local material—some brush—was used to indicate the site, which is now the corner of Santa Barbara and Canon Perdido Streets. The Santa Barbara Presidio was the fourth and last in a string of military sites established between San Diego and Monterey to provide protection for the coast and support for some of the twenty-one missions in Alta California. Lieutenant Ortega, who had accompanied Governor Neve and Father Serra, became first comandante of the Presidio de Santa Barbara. Under his command, the Presidio was

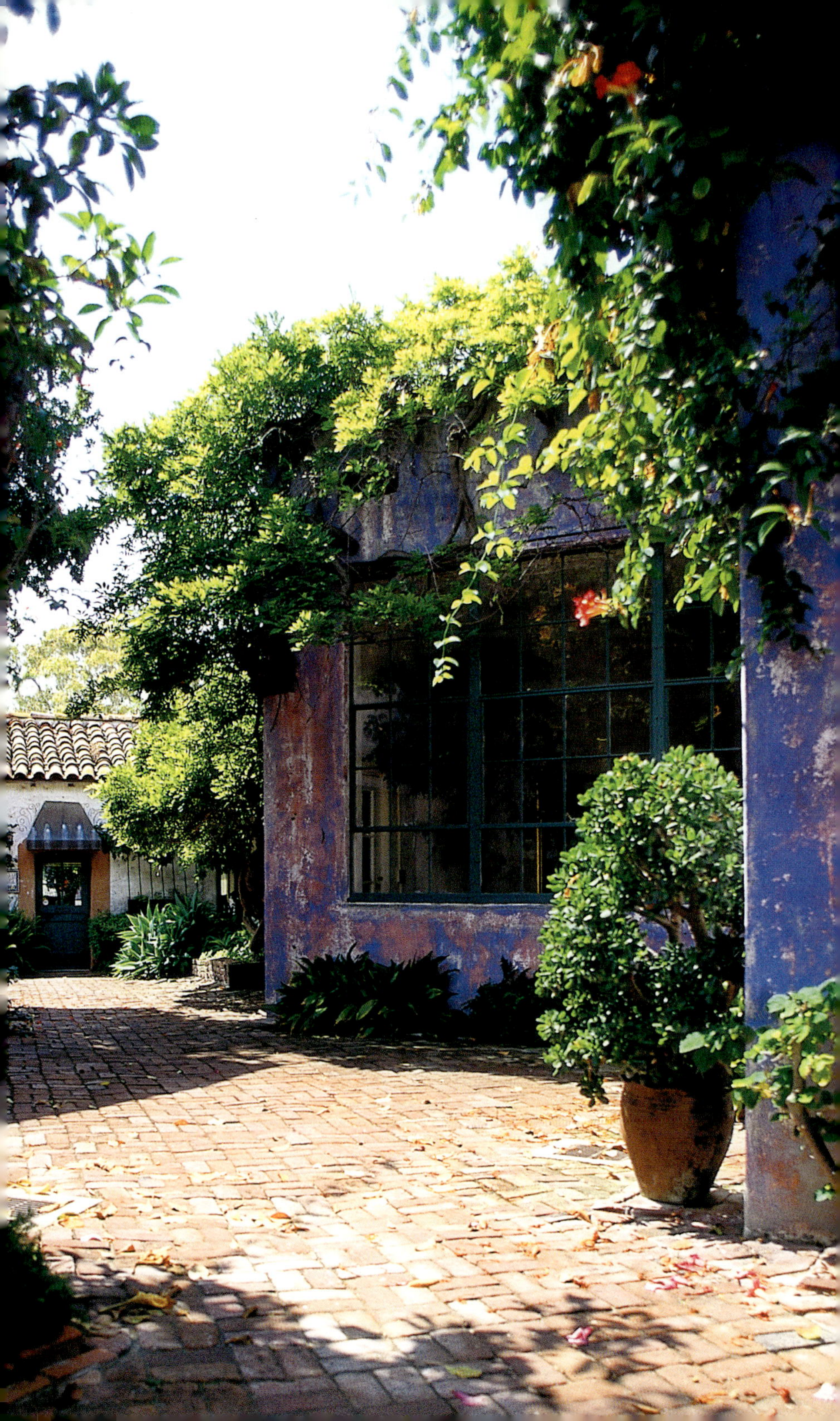

responsible for the protection of all the missions between San Fernando and San Luis Obispo, and the Presidio complex eventually grew to an impressive size. When the Presidio buildings were completed, they had roofs made of terra-cotta—thus the birth of our red-tile city. The Presidio has been authentically reconstructed on the original site at 122-129 E. Canon Perdido Street by the Santa Barbara Trust for Historic Preservation. It includes restored quarters for the soldiers and for the resident padre, a museum, and a picturesque chapel. To pay a visit is truly to step back in time.

Four years after the Presidio was established, the Mission was at last founded by Father Fermin Francisco de Lasuen, Presidente of the California missions. Sadly, Father Serra did not live to see his dream fulfilled; he had died two years earlier. It is said that the early Franciscan padres had unerring wisdom in picking the garden spots along the California coast for their missions. Standing at the Mission on a clear morning and taking in the view towards the ocean, you can appreciate their inspired choice. The location was sufficiently distant from the Presidio to be independent of the fort's military air, and in December 1786, on the feast day of St. Barbara, the site was consecrated.

The "Queen of the Missions," as it has come to be known, had humble beginnings. The first Mass was celebrated under an arbor of tree boughs. A year later, the Chumash Indians, under the command of the padres, built an adobe church with a thatched roof, later tiled with red terra-cotta. Over the years the Mission went through several expansions. By 1820, the Mission had become a beautiful structure whose majesty could be seen from ships passing through our bay. The Mission in 1820 looked almost exactly as it does today, except for the second tower, which was added in 1833. Its sandstone twin towers soon became an icon for sailors, sometimes from faraway lands, confirming that they had at last reached Santa Barbara bay.

The Santa Barbara Mission is much more than a monument to

California's early history; it is also an example of dedicated efforts for preservation and a tribute to the devoted service of the Franciscan padres. Although the towers collapsed during the earthquake of 1925, and were rebuilt shortly afterwards, the service of the Franciscan padres to the faithful has continued without interruption since the Mission's founding in 1786. In the courtyard outside the Mission gurgles a beautiful Moorish fountain, built in 1808, above the lavadero where Indian women once washed their clothes. The interior of the church is spectacularly painted, colorful and light-filled, and contains eighteenth- and nineteenth-century Spanish and Mexican treasures, artifacts, and art. A self-guided tour will take you through a restored padre's cell, the Mission kitchen, the garden, and finally into the cemetery, where four thousand Indians, as well as some prominent Santa Barbarans, are buried. Walk across the wide lawn in front of the Mission and look back toward the mountains for a sweeping view. Easily spotted, the A.C. Postel Memorial Rose Garden offers everyone a great place to stop and smell the roses. The Mission is located about a mile north of downtown, at the corner of Laguna and Los Olivos Streets. Masses are celebrated daily.

The earliest literary mention of Santa Barbara is in Richard Henry Dana's *Two Years before the Mast*, published in 1840. In 1836, Dana anchored in the bay, came ashore, and attended a wedding at the Casa de la Guerra. He describes the impact of seeing the Mission on the hill from the sea and knowing that his ship had reached Santa Barbara. Believe it or not, he also mentions the red-tile roofs of the hundred or so houses that at that time surrounded the Presidio. He writes in detail about the festivities and the hospitality offered by the Presidio's comandante, whose daughter was getting married. So the important things never change. Just as it did then, the Mission still stands as Santa Barbara's most famous landmark, and the red-tile roofs continue to be a defining characteristic of downtown. And of course, Santa Barbara's warm welcome for the traveler is still renowned.

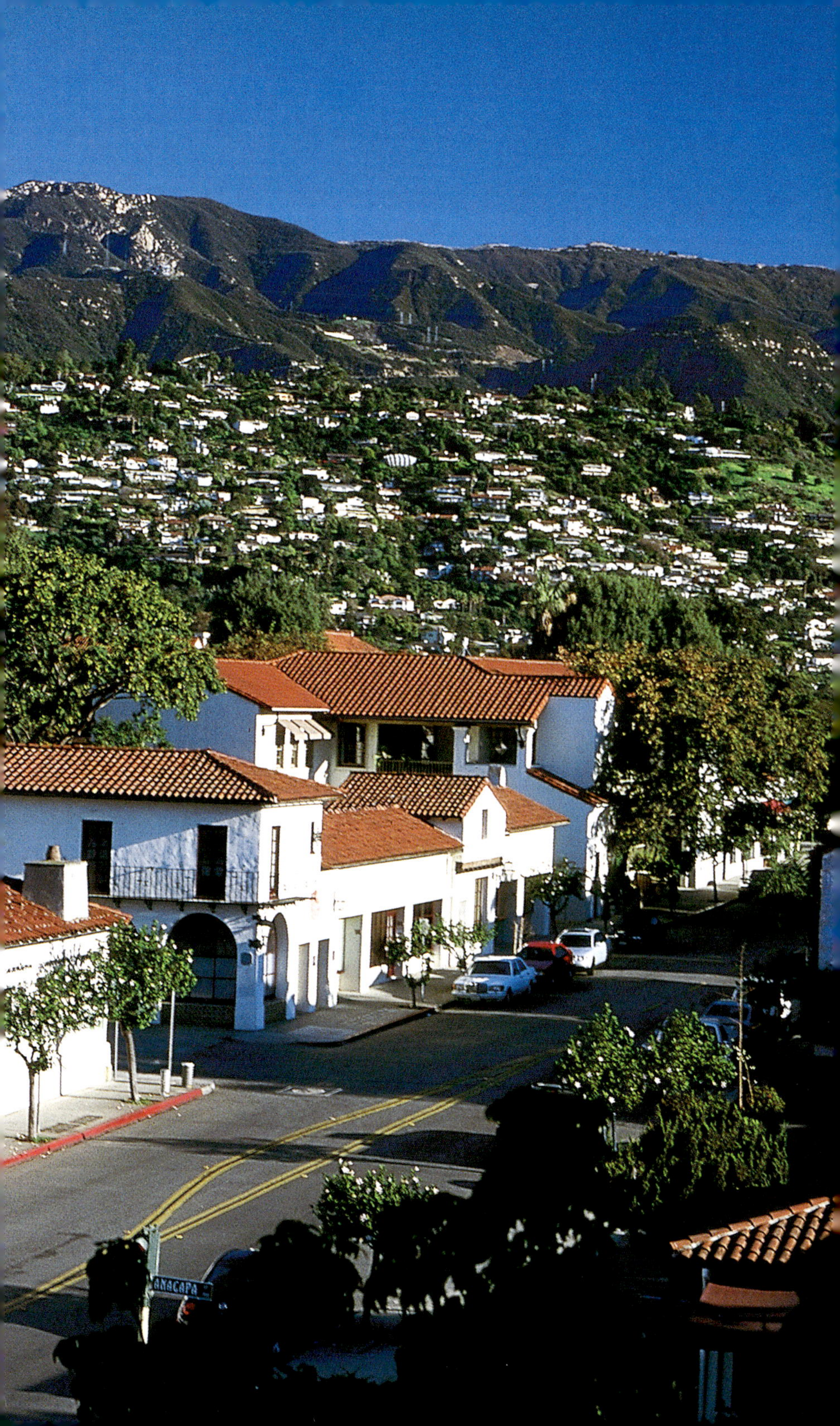
ANACAPA

Navigating Downtown

The De la Guerra house that Dana describes is situated in the heart of present-day downtown. The lawn of nearby De la Guerra Plaza is a great place to start a tour of the historic downtown area. Next to the Plaza, look for the compass incised into the sidewalk near the Santa Barbara News-Press building. Standing before the compass, you can appreciate the idiosyncrasies of Santa Barbara's layout. To begin with, the ocean truly is to the south—not to the west as one would assume in California. Furthermore—and confusing to everyone—our town and its streets are laid out on a diagonal, and the streets are of different lengths. The first city surveyor (1851), one Captain Haley, was the lowest bidder for the job. We've been paying ever since. When his surveying chain broke, the sea-captain-cum-surveyor used leather strings to mend it. But unfortunately, leather stretches on humid days, so his measurements differed from street to street. Before Haley's survey, people had clustered their adobes around the Presidio in a happenstance way. After the streets were constructed, the town's appearance was more orderly. But we still have trouble describing exactly where things are. So Santa Barbarans, when giving directions, often simply say "turn toward the mountains" or "face the ocean." Streets are labeled "east" or "west" depending on which side of State Street they're located on.

Oh, the street names—Cabrillo, Castillo, and Carrillo are so easily mistaken for each other! Be sure to check twice so you won't head to the beach when you're intending to go downtown. Two other notoriously confusing street names are Anapamu and Anacapa. Anapamu runs east/west; Anacapa north/south.

This discussion might be more information than is helpful without a map. Good maps and other visitor's materials can be had at the Visitor Center kiosk on the corner of Garden Street and Cabrillo Boulevard right across from the beach, and the friendly staff there will answer your questions. Be sure to ask for the map of downtown

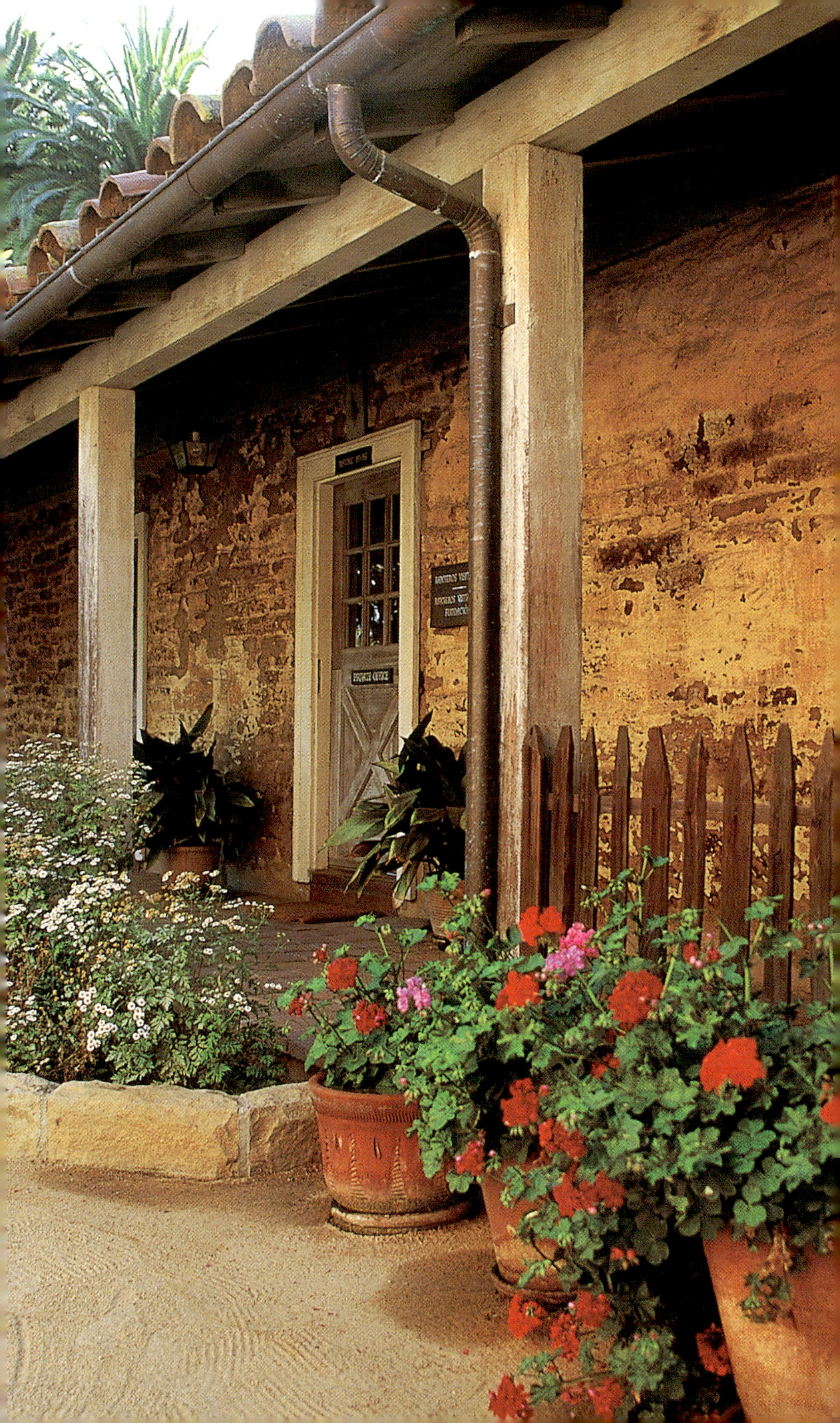

that includes the Sixteen Points of Interest and the self-guided Red Tile Downtown Historic Walking Tour. The present chapter includes an abbreviated version of this sightseeing stroll through the heart of Santa Barbara. If you're ready for a walk at 10 A.M. on a Saturday or Sunday, the best tour in town is sponsored by the Architectural Foundation and costs just $5. On Saturdays, a docent from the Foundation will meet you at the steps in front of City Hall for an informative walk through downtown, the oldest part of the city. On Sundays, their descriptive architectural tour of "uptown" begins at the public library on Anapamu Street.

I like to have a cup of coffee before a tour, so if you haven't had your morning brew yet, stroll around the corner from De la Guerra Plaza to State Street, where you'll find at least three coffee shops within a block. Some consider people-watching from a table at an outdoor cafe a minor sport. You'd be hard pressed to find another small city where you can see folks from so many parts of the world walking by. Tourists flock here to enjoy themselves and each other in a friendly and unhurried manner. We Santa Barbarans like our leisure, and the downtown sidewalk cafes encourage this *dolce far niente*, or "double-distilled sweet idleness," as a visitor to Santa Barbara in 1843 phrased it when he found that "There wasn't a timekeeper in the place."

The small-town atmosphere makes our dress more casual, too. If you see a suit during the daytime, it means the wearer is in a very conservative occupation, or perhaps is from out of town. A couple of restaurants require a coat and tie, but for many locals a pair of flip-flops—beach shoes (in black) constitute formal dress. For the activities listed in this book, comfortable is sufficiently fashionable.

The notion that "things were better before" is age-old. Downtown Santa Barbara has always had its guardians or, to put it mildly, its citizens who are curious, caring, and wary of change. I was amused, in my research, to find this quote:

"The old landmarks and most charming characteristics of Santa Barbara are disappearing before the march of 'improvement,' and though our practical people cannot move the mountains, nor change the scenes, nor spoil the climate, they are doing all they can to despoil the quaint beauty of the place and make it just a commonplace American town."

(The Morning Press, January 3, 1874)

The more things change in Santa Barbara, it seems the more the citizens' sentiments remain the same.

But enough chatting. To see first hand how things have changed yet remained the same, take the self-guided red-tile tour mentioned earlier, or follow me. We've had our coffee; if you've got on your walking shoes, let's begin!

Historical Tour of Downtown

Downtown Santa Barbara, dating from the early 1800s, has some of the most visually delightful buildings of any American city. People who placed a high value on social interaction constructed our first buildings with this purpose in mind, and with a care that comes with working by hand. The spirit of those structures has been appreciated and emulated down to the present. As you walk down the streets and stroll through the paseos, you can see the love and attention that have been lavished on the creation and preservation of our city.

Few residents, and fewer visitors, take the time to see the most remarkable part of old Santa Barbara, just off State Street and within two blocks of De la Guerra Plaza. Within the span of a short walk you can appreciate the history that brought Santa Barbara from the days of the Chumash through the rule of Spain and Mexico to establishment as an early American California city. Along the way, you can see some unique, charming architecture, for the influences of Spain, Mexico, and the Yankees have each left distinctive and colorful marks on the adobes and gardens in the heart of the city. As you follow this tour, please be respectful of the business being conducted

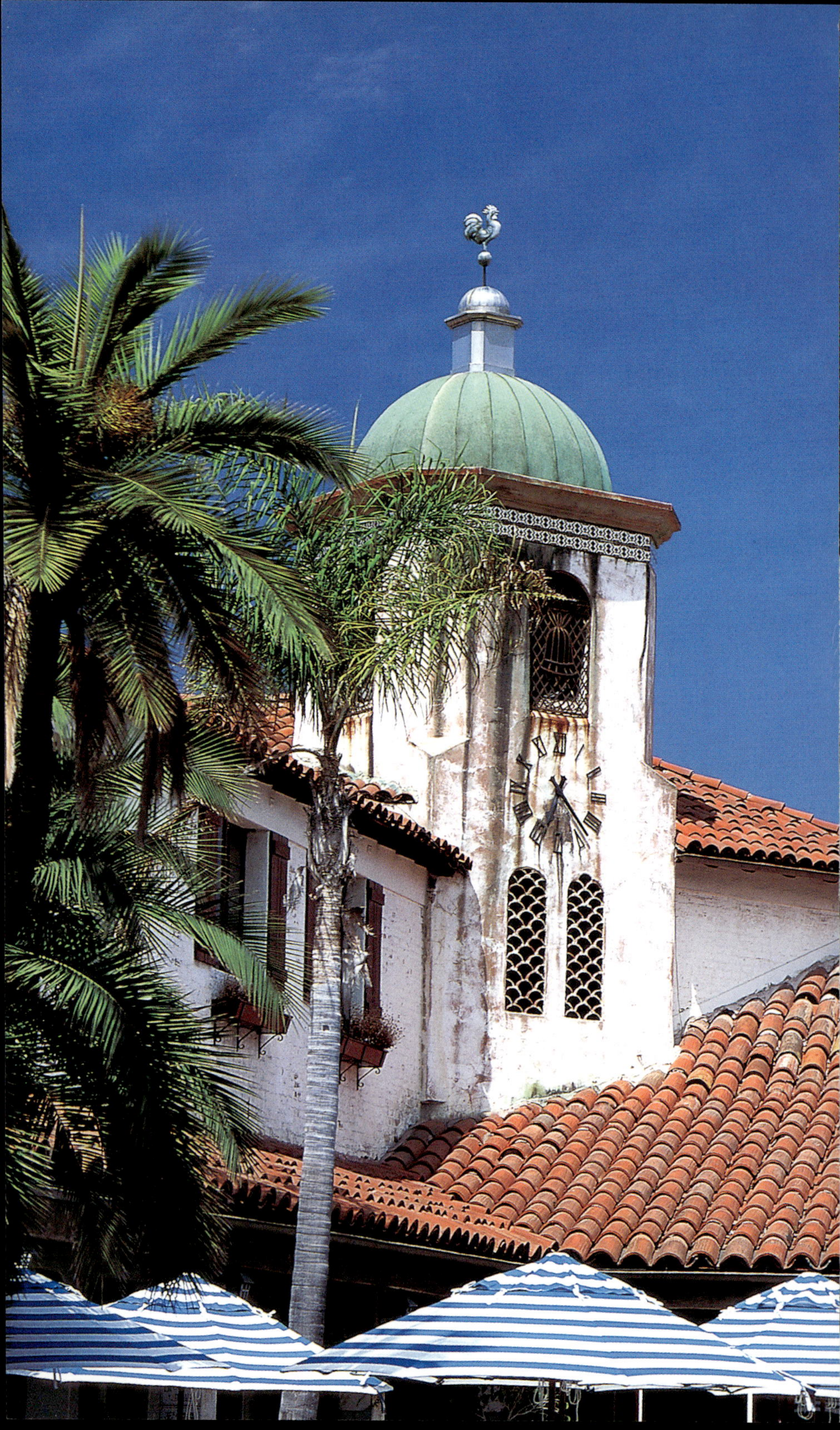

in some of the historic places, and please don't trespass on private property.

Let's begin in De la Guerra Plaza. City Hall stands to the east of the plaza, and the News-Press building is to its south. Across the street to the north you'll see Casa de la Guerra. This old adobe, dating from 1819, is open Thursday through Sunday afternoons. The surrounding yard it is authentically parched, telling of the pioneer era—an odd juxtaposition with the lushness visible almost everywhere else in Santa Barbara today. Consider it a reminder that things weren't always better before.

Adjoining the Casa is lovely El Paseo, opened in 1923. This splendid structure was designed by architect James Osborne Craig, a Scotsman who spent his childhood vacations in Andalusia, Spain. Those must have been wonderful holidays, for remembering them, he designed what has become quintessential Santa Barbara architecture. His vision for El Paseo gave us an enchanting building that, after the 1925 earthquake, served as the model for rebuilding the city in its signature style. El Paseo's charming Spanish courtyard, with its quiet fountain and surrounding shops, apartments, and open-air restaurant, reminds us of a bygone era. The shady walkways are overhung with bougainvillea and orange honeysuckle vines that reach up to trace the wrought-iron balconies and red-tile roofs. A stroll through El Paseo at almost any time evokes nostalgia for old Spain.

Let's continue our stroll by crossing De la Guerra Street on the north side of De la Guerra Plaza. There you'll see the Casa de la Guerra, and then the Orena Adobes just east of the Casa, at 27-39 East De la Guerra. Built in 1849-58, these quaint buildings are now offices and businesses adjoining El Paseo. Continue east to Anacapa Street and cross diagonally to find the Santiago de la Guerra Adobe at 100 East De la Guerra. Next door, the Lugo Adobe (circa 1820), at 114 East De la Guerra Street, is almost hidden at the back of the picturesque Meridian Studios. This studio complex has provided

Presidio Building

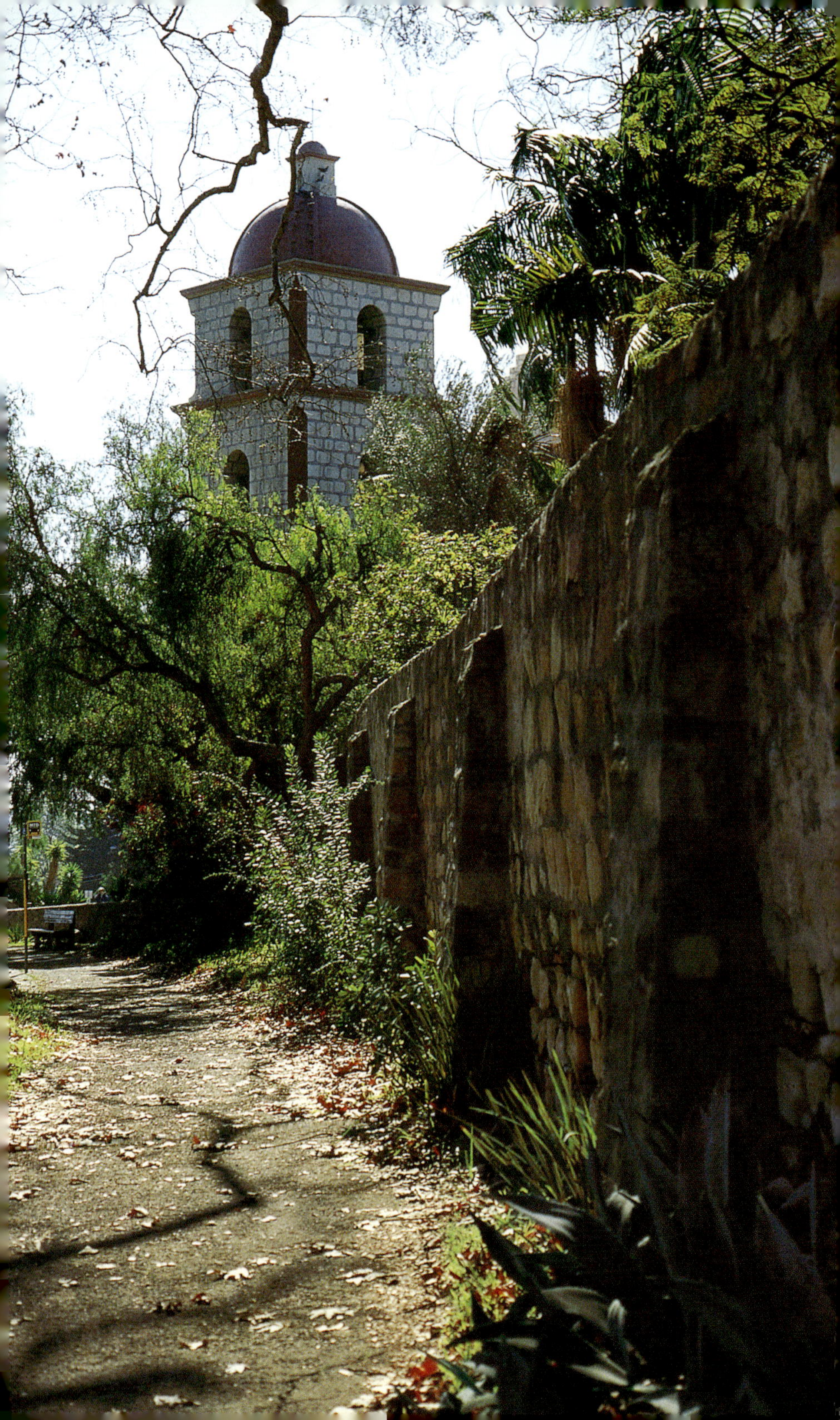

workspaces for artists and architects since its construction. It was designed in 1923 by prominent local architect George Washington Smith, famous for giving Santa Barbara much of its style, and was finished by Carlton Winslow in 1925. The complex's beautiful exterior walls beckon from State Street partly because of their imaginative coloring.

Across De la Guerra Street, to the north of the Meridian Studios, is our shortest and oldest street, Presidio Avenue. If you look up atop the Presidio Building there, you'll see some lovely blue-glazed vases. On the other side of the building is a tranquil, shaded courtyard with a pond.

Care to see Zorro's saddle? It's at the museum—the Santa Barbara Historical Society Museum nearby at 136 E. De la Guerra Street. The black-masked Zorro of television and movie fame is based on the life of a Santa Barbara man. Of course, "Zorro" wasn't his real name (were you expecting him to tell?). But as you peruse our old adobes, can't you just imagine Zorro zipping across the red-tile roofs, taunting the cruel, undeserving aristocrats? Inside the museum building you will also find the Gledhill Library, where books, maps, photos, and audio tapes on Santa Barbara's history are preserved and catalogued.

Around the corner is the handsome Casa de Covarrubias (circa 1817) at 715 Santa Barbara Street. This old adobe, with its 55-foot main room, or sala, has served for nearly 200 years as a great place to host a crowd; the area hums at Fiesta time. Next door is the Historic Adobe, where Los Rancheros Visitadores, an exclusive riding club, has their headquarters. Their first annual spring ride through Santa Barbara's backcountry was held in 1930, and they have been keeping the cowboy tradition alive ever since.

When you've walked enough and want to take a break, turn your steps toward the eclectic restaurants and bakery just a block north at Santa Barbara and Canon Perdido Streets, facing the Presidio. As you enjoy your pick-me-up, you might consider and sympathize with those who through the years have battled to retain Santa Barbara's leisurely pace and hospitable grace, and protect its beautiful landmarks from being "struck down and ground out of existence by the piston-thrust and the great steel wheels of the monster vehicle of Progress" (Santa Barbara, Tierra Adorada, 1930).

One of the telling landmarks of the battle with "Progress" stands on the east side of the 1200 block of State Street. The Granada Theatre, at 1216 State, is one of the few buildings that survived the devastating earthquake of 1925. Constructed just one year before the quake, this looming structure has an ultra-baroque façade, while its three remaining sides are utterly blank and boxy. Cross the street to get a good look at this "high rise," which is an anomaly for Santa Barbara. Does it remind you of a woman who's trying to hide something by wearing too much makeup? Now imagine how our downtown might have looked if the planned but (happily) never constructed neighboring buildings had taken their expected places flanking the Granada. This theater, the tallest building in the city, is eight stories high. It was not subject to the laws put in place in 1925 by the Architectural Review Board, which decreed after the earthquake that no buildings can rise more than four stories (excluding decorative towers). That's why Santa Barbara's architecture has an intimate feeling that humans seem to crave. Thankfully, on many occasions the "monster vehicle of Progress" has spared Santa Barbara because of the willingness of its citizens to care, and to cry out.

The Riviera

I want to tell you about a Santa Barbara theater with a past that's not located downtown. (See chapter 3 for descriptions of downtown theaters.) Located far above the city's lights, the Riviera Theatre is my favorite place to see a movie. It has comfortable seats and good sound, and the movies are rarely the Hollywood "blockbusters", more often, thoughtful and beautiful art films. The parking lot and steps up to the theater offer a stellar view of Santa Barbara and the ocean.

The Riviera was so named because the early fashionable residents of our city thought that they'd found a haven as beautiful as the Riviera of France "without the strain of having to go to Europe." But before it became such a fashionable part of town, this hillside was called "Hawley's Folly," since the owner, Mr. Hawley, had paid good money for a desolate, treeless hillside that the prevailing public transportation—the horse-drawn streetcar—could not climb. Horse-drawn cars could travel only from the beach to the Mission, a fairly flat course. But with the advent of electric streetcars, which first rolled down State Street in 1896, traveling up that Riviera hillside became a possibility. Two decades later, the possibility became a reality when the line was extended from the Mission to the Riviera. Today, we still use Alameda Padre Serra, which was graded originally for the streetcar, as a crosstown route.

The buildings that now comprise the Riviera Theatre and nearby office quadrant were built to be a school in 1913. The Normal School, as it was called then, was able to move from downtown to this new campus on the Riviera once the electric streetcar line was in place. You can still see the last streetcar passenger shelter at the corner of Pedregosa Street and Lasuen Road near the theater. The school eventually became the University of California at Santa Barbara, now a sprawling campus in Goleta, 13 miles to the north.

When the Normal School moved up to the Riviera, convenient housing was needed for faculty, so quarters were built near the campus. When the buildings were no longer used for housing, they were converted into a hotel. Today, El Encanto Hotel is famous, like most of the Riviera, for its magnificent views. One of the nicest vistas is from the hotel's outdoor dining deck—an expansive panorama of the city with the ocean and the Channel Islands as the backdrop.

Welcoming the Stranger

Santa Barbara was a tourist destination before the phrase was invented—partly the result of a publication distributed by Southern Pacific Railroad in the late 1800s. Their publicist, Charles Nordhoff, also wrote a series of articles for Harper's Magazine on California, with the aim of attracting travelers and settlers. In one of those installments, titled "Southern California for Invalids," he decreed that Santa Barbara had the best climate anywhere on the West Coast. This remark had an inspiring effect on our city's development. By the late 1800s, "invalids" were arriving daily, first by stagecoach and soon after by steamship—sometimes as many as 100 a day—and finally, by the newly completed railroad. Santa Barbara's reputation as a "Mecca for the Moribund" was amplified by publicity, but the Indians had known long before of the area's curative effects. Learning from the native Chumash, early inhabitants enjoyed the healing powers of the local hot springs and their waters. And, like a ripple, the word spread.

One of those mineral springs survives today: Montecito Hot Springs. Others, no longer available to us, include Burton's Mound sulfur springs, near an original Indian settlement at West Beach, and Veronica Springs, which the Indians knew for the water's mildly laxative effects. Veronica Spring Water became famous and was bottled and sold at drugstores throughout the country from 1880 to 1928. Sadly, Burton's Mound was cemented over by Mr. Potter when he built his namesake hotel across from the beach in 1902. He and many of his guests despised the sulfur smell, and he declared that "Some of the people who aren't sick should be enjoying the place, too."

The Cemetery

Looking around Santa Barbara, you might think its people are the healthiest in the world. In fact, our obsession with health is a subject for comedy elsewhere. But despite the age-old yearning for the fountain of youth, everything eventually has to end. As a fitting close to this chapter on history, I suggest a trip to the Santa Barbara Cemetery at the corner of Channel Drive and East Cabrillo Boulevard. Even here, Santa Barbara has a certain style. Take a peaceful walk among the eclectic array of monuments and appreciate the poetry of love and loss. The viewing benches that invite contemplation of the vast Pacific from the bluff are an exquisite and considerate touch. It's rumored that certain rich and famous folks who didn't even live in Santa Barbara chose this place as their burial site. It's not hard to imagine why. George Washington Smith designed the chapel. After his death in 1930, he was interred there, and his widow commissioned the famous Mexican painter Alfredo Ramos Martinez to decorate the chapel's interior. Many of the "greats" from Santa Barbara's past are buried in this cemetery, and even if you don't recognize their names, you get a sense of who they were and the values of their time when you encounter their tombstones. The inscriptions and the style and placement of the memorials hold insights into the personal history of those they honor. If we are wise, we silently understand their lessons.

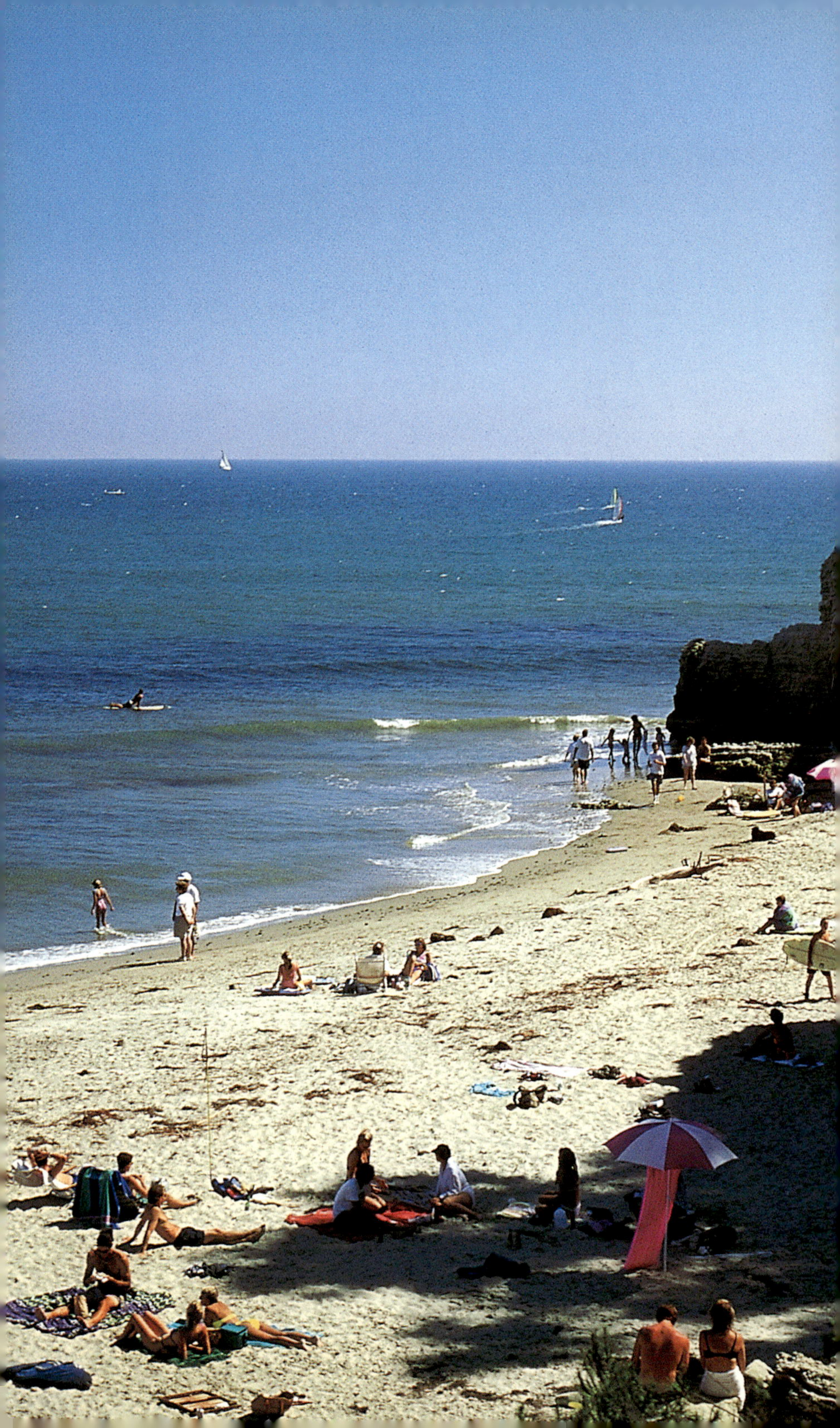

The Ocean and the Beach
Chapter Two

Perfect weather pours down on Santa Barbara making almost every day a good day to head for the surf. Our south-facing location and open bay provide a playground of wide sands under gently swaying palm trees. And the wonders of the ocean are right at our city's feet—the beach starts where State Street ends. Here, at the start of Stearns Wharf, where the Friendship Fountain's bronze dolphins leap into the air, the fun begins. The shoreline unfurls three miles to the east, nine miles to the west, and the most natural thing in the world is to take off your shoes right here in the sand and begin a beach walk.

An easy way to enjoy the beach and the sea air without even taking off your shoes is to join the bikes, roller skaters, and joggers along the paved path that winds for two miles eastward alongside the sand. If you choose this walkway, please note the signs that encourage cooperation among the vari-

Ledbetter Beach

ous modes of travel so traffic can flow safely. You may opt for a leisurely stroll. But if you want to bicycle or skate, rental equipment is available nearby at the corner of State and Cabrillo streets. The path takes the most scenic route, paralleling the water, for a mile. Then it crosses over East Cabrillo Boulevard at Milpas Street, allowing a closer look at some of the well-manicured beachfront hotels. Just before reaching Milpas Street, if you look away from the ocean, you'll notice a gigantic, angular, rainbow-hued sculpture on the grass between Calle Puerto Vallarta and Cabrillo Boulevard. Herbert Bayer, a resident of Santa Barbara and an influential designer who trained at the Bauhaus school in Germany in the 1920s, made this playful arch for us. It seems perfectly suited as the entrance to the land of the carefree, and since it is on park land, the surrounding grass is often the site for frisbee or hackey-sack games or other gatherings that require an uninterrupted stretch of lawn.

As you progress along the beachside path, you'll cross Los Ninos Drive and round a curve, passing the zoo. Then the path makes a long swing around Andree Clark Bird Refuge, a placid freshwater lagoon and sanctuary for birds. On the way, you might want to stop for a rest while you watch the high-spirited volleyball games at the end of East Beach, across from the zoo.

All along this two-mile track you can witness humanity at play or celebration: kite-flying, soccer games, and football scrimmages, and on weekends, weddings at the beach. Out on the water you'll see sailboats, surfers, wind surfers, rowers, parasailers, and kayakers. Along this same palm-lined boulevard, every Sunday and on a few other holidays, the Art and Crafts Beach Show sets the stage for 250 local artists to display and sell their art. Look for them along the sidewalk between State Street and Calle Caesar Chavez from 10 A.M. to 5 P.M.

If you're not up for traveling along the waterfront under your own steam, Santa Barbara has thoughtfully provided the Downtown-

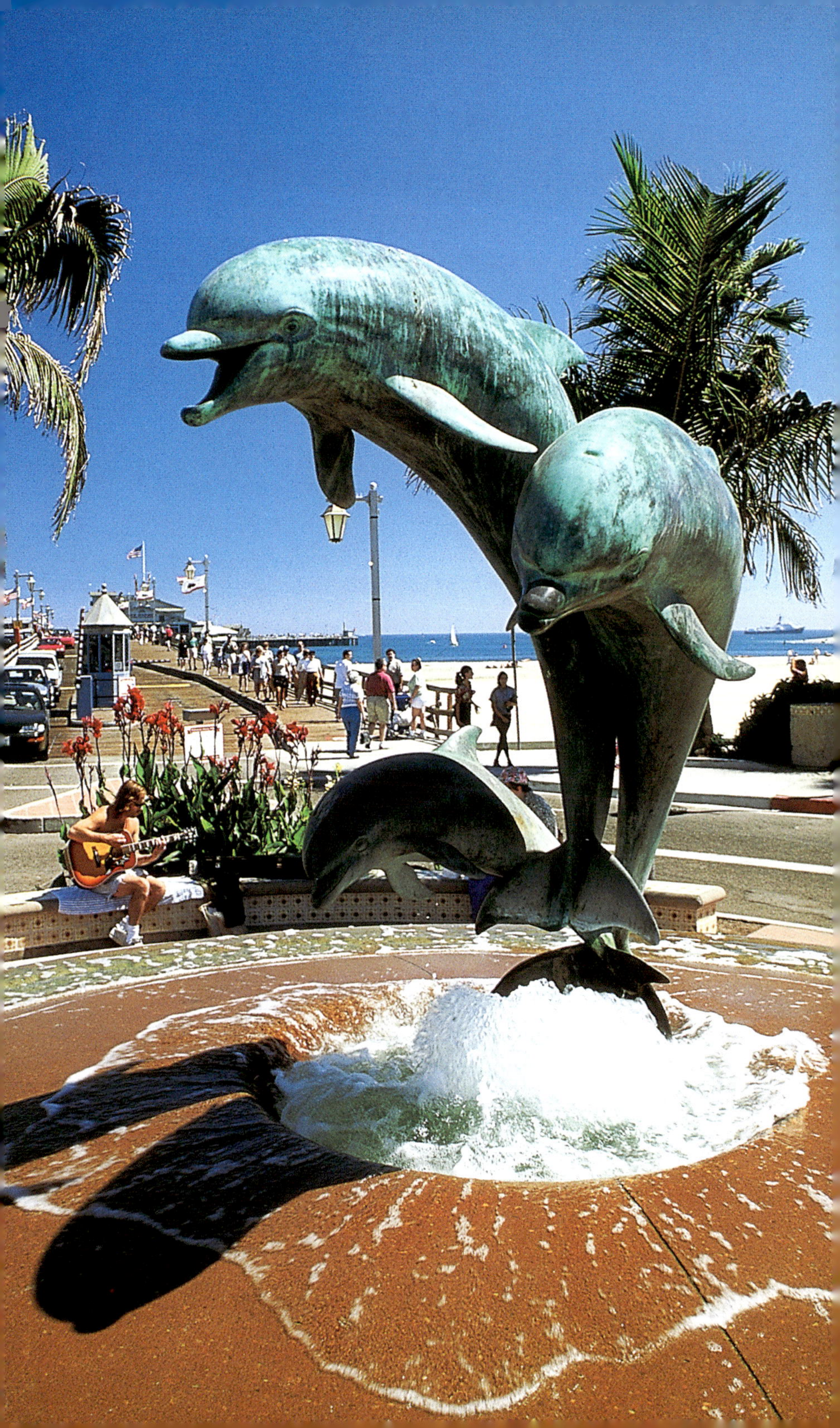

Waterfront Shuttle, a comfortable bus that travels between the harbor and the zoo, departing every 20 or 30 minutes from 10:30 A.M. to 5 P.M. For a quarter you can get on the bus at any of the marked benches along both sides of Cabrillo Boulevard and ride to any destination along this route. (An additional downtown route runs from the beach up State Street as far as the Arlington Theater.)

Also on Cabrillo Boulevard, at the corner of Garden Street, is the friendly and informative Santa Barbara Visitor Center. The staff are glad to give you free maps, directions, and advice on how to make your visit even more fun. Public restrooms and parking are adjacent. This is a good place to park your car if you've been driving. Across the street from the Visitor Center the hand-carved antique carousel, an old-fashioned work of art from 1916, gives kids and their parents the ride of their lives.

For a closer look at any of the water sports, check in at the breakwater, at the west end of the harbor, one mile west of State Street, to rent a kayak, a surfboard, or a boat. If a stress-free ocean adventure is more to your liking, inquire about a local cruise; there are several willing captains with their trusty boats ready to entertain you at sea for a day, an afternoon, or a sunset cruise. Some of your choices include: the Condor Express (882-0088), the Rachel G (969-5217), the Double Dolphin (962-2826), and Sunset Kidd Charters (962-8222). The waters off the coast of Santa Barbara play host to an astounding array of marine life. Among the most exciting are the dolphins and whales, and the aforementioned boats can take you out to see them. Between December and the end of April each year, as many as 25,000 gigantic gray whales migrate through Santa Barbara waters on their way to Alaska. Blue and humpback whales are sighted during the summer and fall and dolphins can be seen year-round. Or if a day of ocean fishing is your idea of the perfect vacation, see the folks at Sea Landing Sports Fishing, near Cabrillo and Bath Streets. Through Island Packers, who set out from Ventura, you can arrange

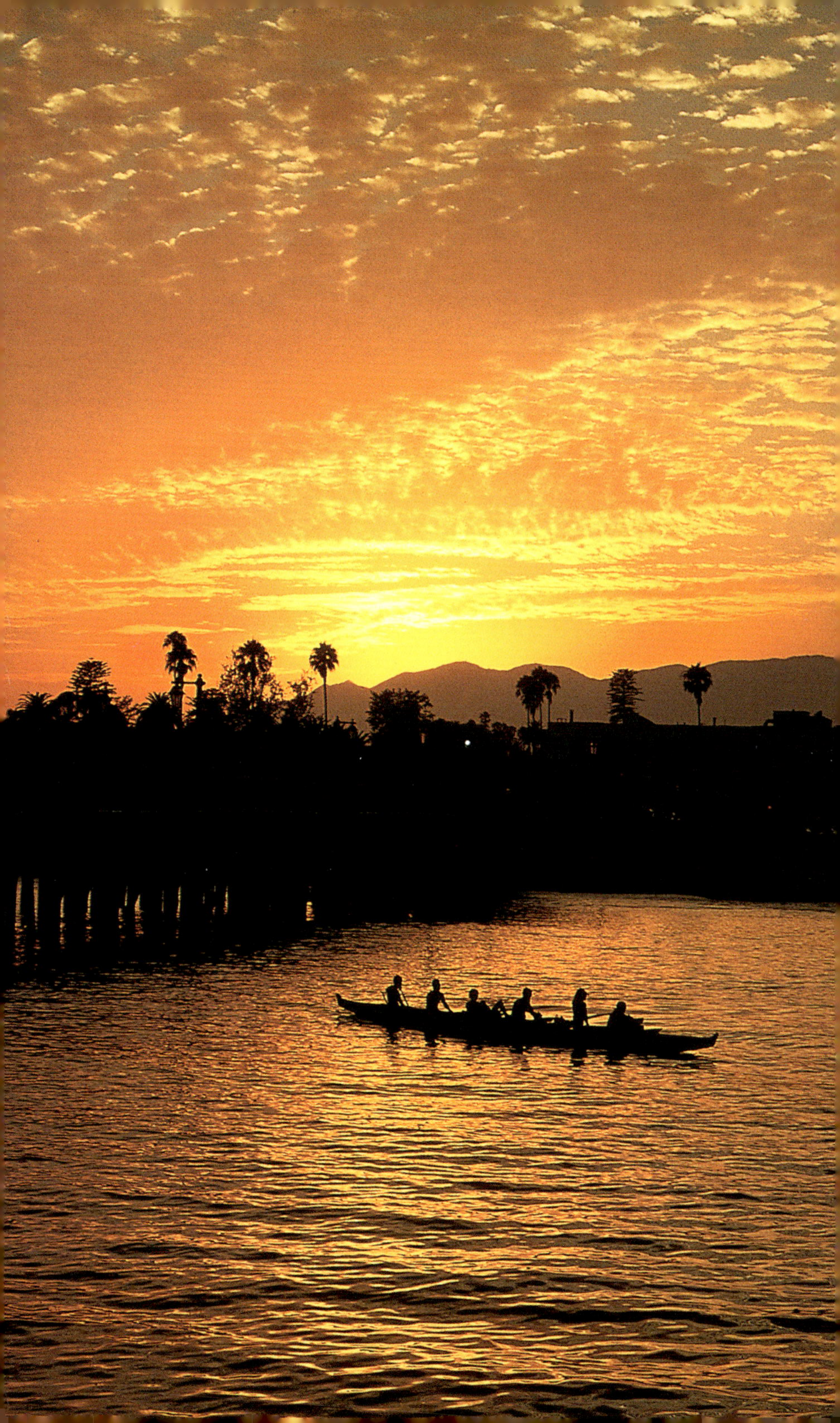

to travel to the Channel Islands, 22 miles offshore, and camp overnight.

A fairly new addition to the beachfront, near the bike path just east of the Dolphin Fountain, is the skateboard park, Skater's Point. Watching swarms of skateboarders thrashing and grinding through the concrete loops, waves, and curves makes for an interesting spectator sport indeed. The park is open to anyone who has the required safety equipment: helmet, knee pads, and elbow pads.

Beaches for Swimming and Beachcombing

For some, the ultimate in relaxation is simple: a good place to lie on the sand, listen to the surf, and look up at the sky as seagulls wheel overhead. No matter what your pleasure, Santa Barbara beaches have something for everyone. Allow me to offer some tips for your day at the beach.

Santa Barbara unfortunately has a pollution problem with creek runoff, and when there is an advisory or a beach closure due to increased bacterial counts, signs are posted on the sand so no one will accidentally swim in polluted water. The Santa Barbara County Public Health Department's Environmental Health Services agency monitors and reports on the water conditions weekly, and you can get safety information for all area beaches by calling the county beach advisory hotline (681-4949). A more detailed report, including data for each beach, is available at the website www.sbcphd.org/ehs/ocean. The county has 20 beaches, so if one or two have advisories, there are still lots of choices. Oh, and don't forget your sunscreen!

One of my favorite places to swim is just a mile east of State Street, between East and Butterfly Beaches. East Beach is the wide sandy shore across from the Bird Refuge; Butterfly Beach is secluded beneath the cliffs near the Biltmore Hotel. I like swimming out a ways and looking back at the shore and the cliffs for a view of our coastline. When I'm gazing across the water and sand to the far-away

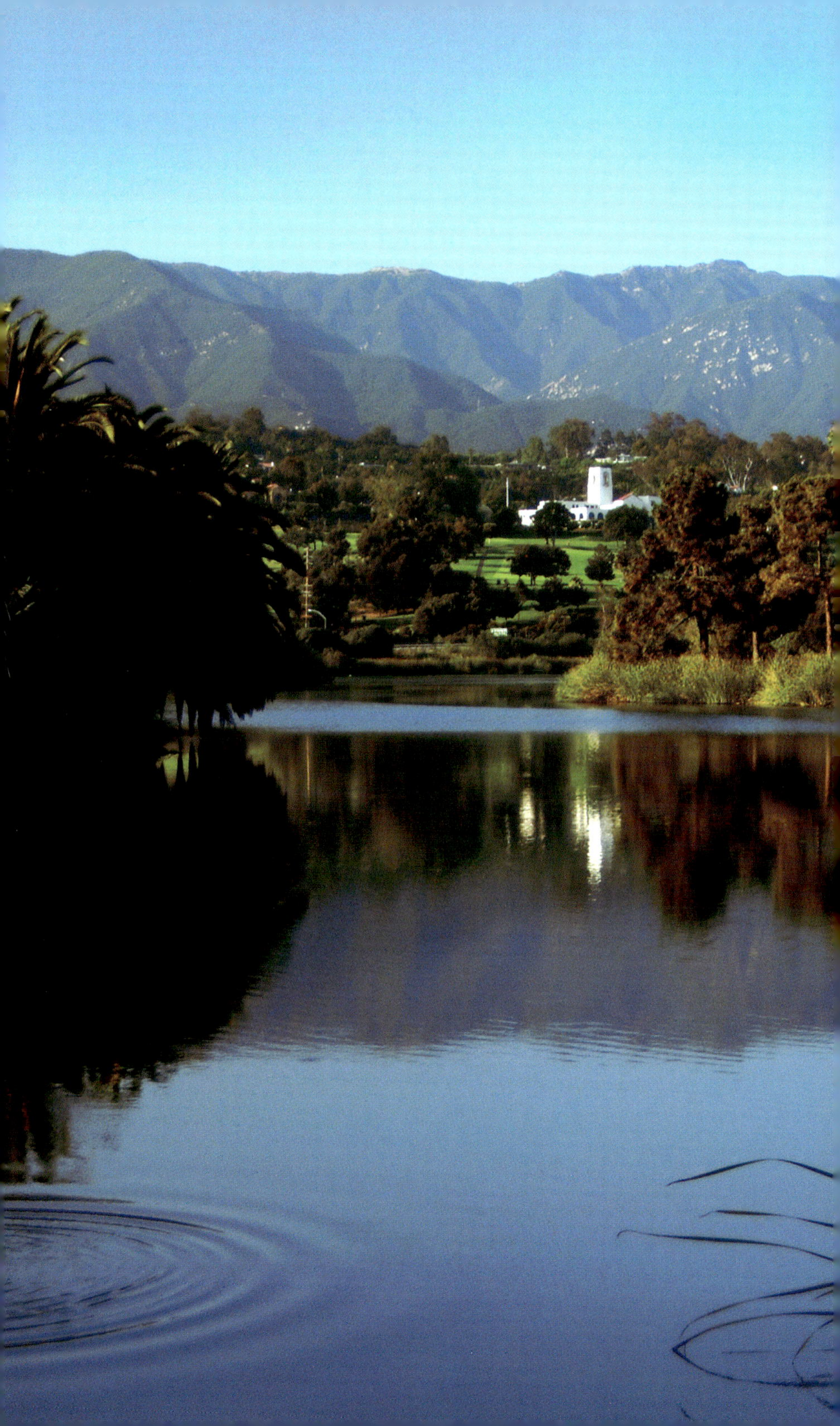

mountains, everything looks peaceful, and all is right with the world. Another great swimming area is just west of the harbor. Located across the street from Santa Barbara City College, Ledbetter Beach Park, at Shoreline and Alta Loma Drive, offers superb people-watching conditions as well as picnic tables, palm trees, and bathrooms with showers to rinse off the sand. Surfers sometimes find easy waves around the point at Ledbetter Beach. Should your quest be a table with a glass of wine right on the beach, look no further than the Shoreline Cafe at Ledbetter Beach Park. They also have a sunny deck with umbrellas. Between the restaurant and the neighboring harbor, a string of brightly colored catamarans lie on the shore, patiently awaiting their owners and the next trip out to sea.

Just 12 miles to the south, in the friendly town of Carpinteria, you'll find "The World's Safest Beach" at the foot of Linden Avenue. Carpinteria Beach is a favorite with families because of its long sandy slope into the water. To get there, drive south on 101, exit at Linden Avenue, and take a right onto the main street, Linden Avenue, which will take you directly to the beach entrance. You'll find all the amenities here: sports rentals, restrooms, and often a lifeguard.

Meanwhile, back in Santa Barbara, close to the harbor and right on the sand, is a wonderful historic outdoor pool, Los Baños del Mar, for those who do laps. The 50-meter, beautifully tiled pool at 401 Shoreline Drive is open to the public year-round. Next door is a children's wading pool, heated and available from May to September. Call 966-6110 for hours and more information.

If you decide to make sandcastle building your sport for the day, the best sand seems to be near East Beach. For a bit of cross-training, you could combine castle-building with watching beach volleyball players. East Beach's sixteen nets are in nearly constant use by volleyball players who have gusto, grace, and such skill that they may be our next Olympic champs. Here, less then a mile from the heart of downtown, the panorama of kids, umbrellas, sunbathers, and ex-

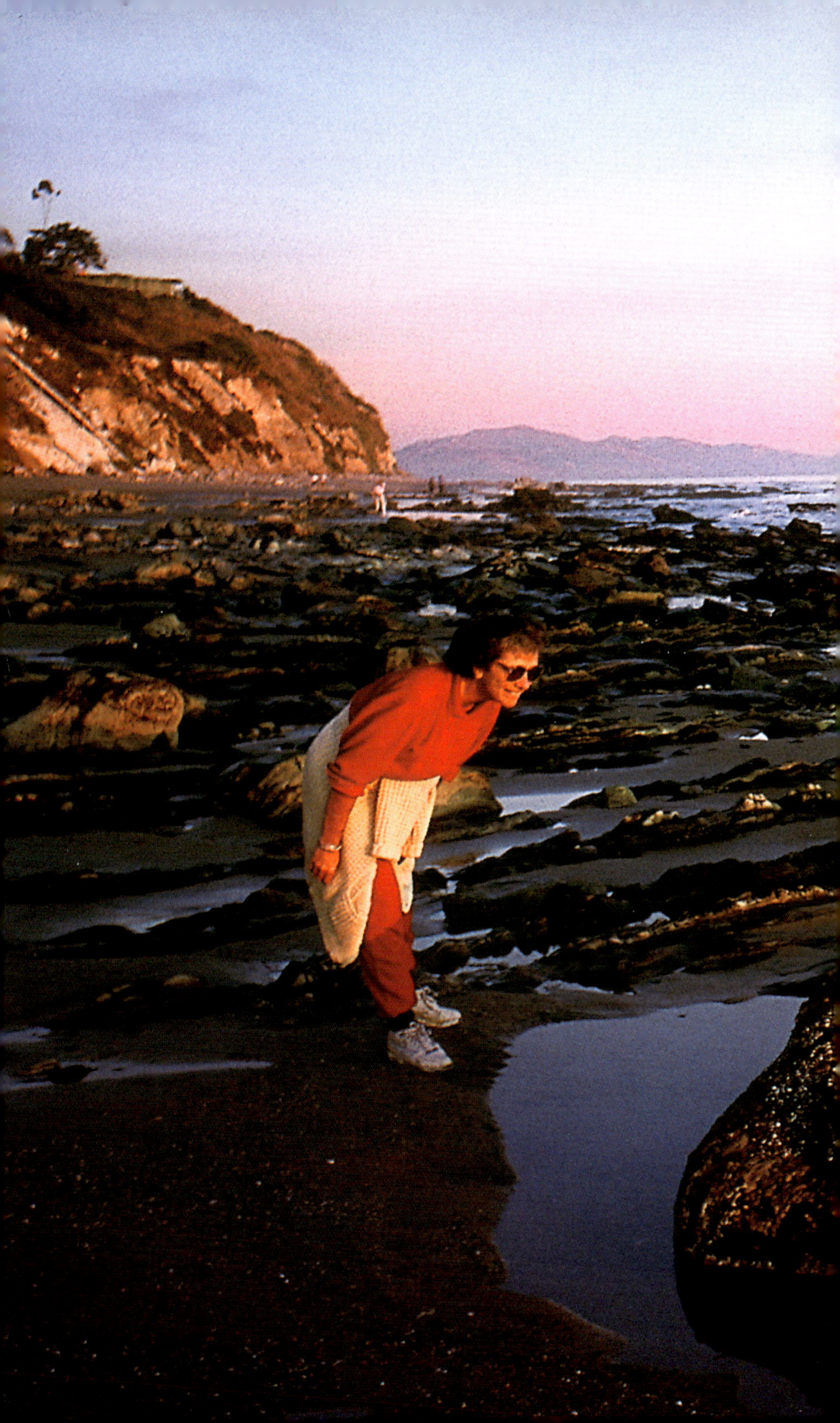

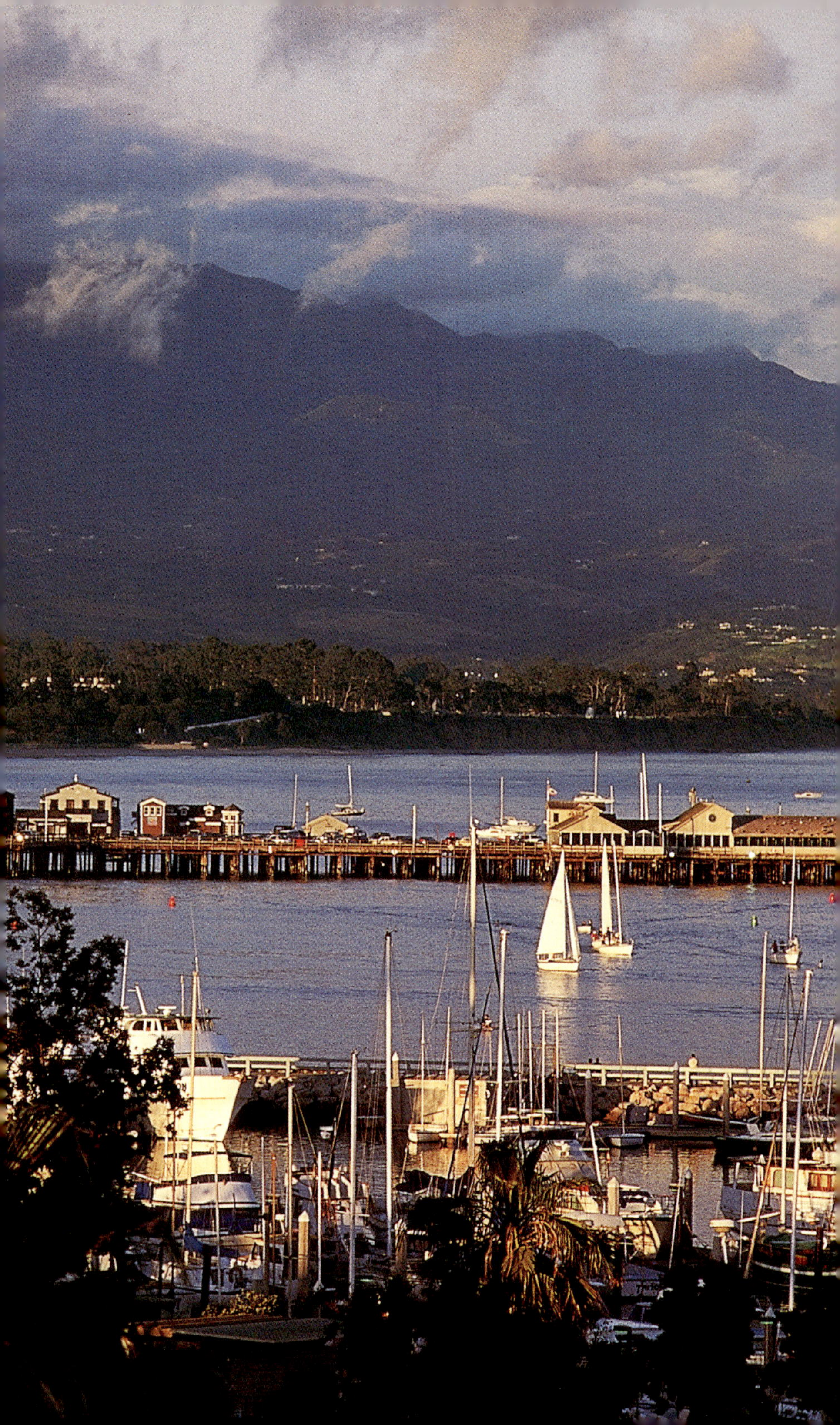

tremely fit youth playing volleyball on the sand presents the epitome of Southern California lifestyle.

Tide Pooling and the Marine Museums

Exploring tide pools is fun for all ages and requires no equipment—all you need for a fascinating look at marine life is a beach with a few rocks and a low tide. Check the newspaper for the tide schedule. There are two low tides on most days, and the most convenient low tides are usually during the winter.

When the remodeled Sea Center reopens on Stearns Wharf in 2004, visitors will once again be able to touch live sea creatures in a recreated living tide pool, or take a video tour of the underwater ocean life around the Channel Islands. Another exceptional educational possibility is at Arroyo Burro County Beach (aka Hendry's Beach, 2981 Cliff Drive). The interactive exhibits and special weekend programs there offer a chance to find out more about the greater watershed of the coastal range behind Santa Barbara. And at the breakwater, next to the harbor, one can learn about the history of sailing at the Maritime Museum, 113 Harbor Way. The museum also offers virtual sport fishing, a working periscope, and a free treasure map for kids.

A Scenic Run on the Sand

Like to run? You have a choice of several one-to-six-mile runs along the sand, beginning where State Street meets the beach. At low tide you can run on packed sand, which most runners prefer. Check the tide schedule, because at high tide the sand around some of the points may be under water.

First, get to the beach. Walk, ride your bike, park your car, or get off the bus near the Dolphin Fountain at State Street, walk down to the sand anywhere by the wharf, and start running east. For a magnificent three-mile course, run eastward from the wharf to Biltmore

Beach; running there and back gives you a level six miles on packed sand. You'll pass families playing in the surf, then the volleyball nets on East Beach, and finally, the secluded area called Butterfly Beach, where Montecito begins.

Rounding a stony point, you'll come upon a great sandy beach across the street from the Four Seasons Biltmore, one of the area's oldest and most beautiful hotels. Constructed in 1927, the Biltmore made an auspicious choice in having its gardens designed by one of Santa Barbara's great landscape architects, Lockwood de Forest. He was also responsible for creating the grounds and gardens of some of Santa Barbara's most lovely estates. You'll see his influence in other parts of the city as well—landscape design that gives preference to natural effects, and native plantings that allow the garden to seamlessly meld into its surroundings. The larger setting for the Biltmore garden includes the vast Pacific Ocean to the south, making it a paradise of blue and green. Also here, under its distinctive pink towers, is the Coral Casino, a prestigious local beach and cabana club and one of the few places in Santa Barbara where you might actually see a tuxedo (though they're usually sighted in the evenings, when runners aren't around).

To enjoy a longer run on the beach, try the stretch from Ledbetter Beach west six miles to More Mesa Beach. Again, remember to check the tide tables to find out when you can run on hard-packed sand. Along this course you'll pass the private Hope Ranch Beach—the sand at the edge of one of America's most luxurious residential communities. If a prepared surface is more to your liking, try the track and field at Santa Barbara City College, across from the beach at Shoreline Drive and Loma Alta. It offers an optional uphill finish through the stadium bleachers.

Boogie Boarding at Bates Beach

You'll need to drive a little to get to Bates Beach, but once you

arrive, you'll appreciate the long and open sandy beach that's less crowded than the ones closer to downtown. It's in the same neighborhood as the famous surfing spot, Rincon Point. The waves at Bates Beach are often gentle and sweeping—perfect for boogie boarding or body surfing, and I've seen dolphins here playing in the waves close to shore. To get to Bates Beach, drive south on 101 from Santa Barbara about 14 miles and look for the Bates Road exit, which leads directly to the beach parking lot. Since this location is a short drive from town and then a three-minute walk down a path to the sand from the parking lot, sun worshipers often come for the day, carrying down their supplies of food, drink, music, books, and homemade shade. There are restroom facilities. Please remember that alcohol is not allowed on any beach or park in Santa Barbara, and dogs must be on a leash. Of course you'll take home with you anything you bring along and, for good karma, pack up any litter someone else might have missed. In Santa Barbara "acting like you own the place" means just that.

A Beach Picnic

Why not watch the sun dip into the Pacific Ocean as you celebrate a birthday, Valentine's Day, a friendship, or the long days of summer with a beach picnic? And for a memorable dinner picnic at the beach, why not plan to watch the sun set and then stay to see the moon rise? With delicious food and some of the best views on earth, this is an indulgence you can afford. Choose the spot and the time, after checking your tide guide and the almanac, published in most newspapers. A low tide and a full moon are the best reservations with nature.

Picnics can be as rustic or as elegant as you please. If all you want to do is to eat outdoors where the little ones can be themselves at the "table," you won't need much more than a blanket, sandwiches, and drinks. On Sundays and holidays, lots of Santa Barbara families bring food to share and enjoy a congenial, leisurely and casual meal at the beach or in a park. A prime location for a midday or sunset picnic is Hendry's Beach (Arroyo Burro County Beach Park). Good locations to grill are East Beach or Shoreline Park; at both places you can sizzle your dinner while you listen to the surf.

Grab your most artistic tablecloth, and put your eating utensils in a big basket. Fill that basket with your favorite restaurant meal—most restaurants will be pleased to provide items on their menu packed to go if you call a day in advance. Or gather the ingredients yourself at one of Santa Barbara's many gourmet delis. Often they're located in grocery stores, such as the wonderland of groceries, Ralphs, near downtown at the corner of Carrillo and De la Vina Streets, or Gelson's grocery store at 3305 State Street. Or step into Pierre Lafond's upscale deli, which has three locations: in the Paseo Nuevo, at the corner of De la Guerra and State Street; at 516 State Street; and in Montecito, at 516 San Ysidro Road. You can get everything you need for a picnic, including the basket, at Trader Joe's at 29 South Milpas Street by the beach.

Gathering picnic supplies is as good an excuse as any to visit one of the wonderful bakeries that dot Santa Barbara's streets. A few of my favorites: D'Angelos at 25 W. Gutierrez, Our Daily Bread at 831 Santa Barbara Street, and the Aficionado at 10 East Carrillo near State Street. Once you've got your fruit, cheese, bread, or other nibbles and something to drink, if you're with friends or someone special, the glorious location should take care of the rest. Have fun!

Water Sports at the Beach

Santa Barbara's winning combination of climate, ocean, and geology supports a world of outdoor diversions, active as well as passive, and some of the most exciting are at the beach. One sport I find inspiring to watch is outrigger-canoe paddling. Stroking strongly and rhythmically, those paddlers are a wholly majestic sight as they glide into the sunset away from the beach. Most evenings you can watch them as they enter the water between Stearns Wharf and the breakwater in their long tropical-looking canoes. The Outrigger Club and the Parks and Recreation Department have joined forces to offer free lessons every Sunday from 10 A.M. to noon. Call 969-5595 for information.

Kayaks, too, are a great way to get an upper-body workout while exploring the peaceful shoreline and observing the diverse natural life in and around our waters. Kayaks can be rented at Paddle Sports, located at the breakwater. During the summer, they often set up a kayak rental spot down on the sand between Stearns Wharf and the breakwater. Call 899-4925 for rental information. You can rent single or double kayaks for an all-day trip, if you're an experienced kayaker, or for two hours, which is more than enough time at the paddle if you're new to the sport. If this is a first time for you, know that kayaking is easy to learn. The renters can give you advice before you set out to sea. Paddle along the shore, around the wharf, or into the harbor, but please find out the rules of the waterways before you set out. In or outside of the harbor, it's possible to find your craft facing a big boat that has less maneuverability than you do!

Local pleasure sailors have a tradition called Wet Wednesdays, sponsored by the Santa Barbara Yacht Club. There are yacht races on Wednesday afternoons between May and October. Look out to the horizon near the harbor to see sails of many colors and sizes skirting along the breeze. And if you'd like to try some sailing yourself, call the Sailing Center of Santa Barbara, 965-0509. And then there's parasailing, and its close relative, kite surfing—two hybrids that combine surfing and sailing. Learning to maneuver a wind-sailing board requires a little effort, especially on windy days. But if you've got a wet suit, why not learn? If you've never surfed, try boogie boarding, which is surfing with a lightweight foam board. For a swimmer it's easy to learn, and it gives you a taste of the thrill of catching a wave.

This area of the California coast is heaven for surfers. Although the Rincon is the famous surf spot, others include Ledbetter Beach, near City College off the point; Padero Lane, north of Carpinteria; Coal Oil Point, near the University of California at Santa Barbara campus at Goleta; and, a little farther north, El Capitan and Refugio, both of which are Santa Barbara County beaches.

The Wharf and the Breakwater

Stearns Wharf, the wooden pier extending into the sea from the foot of State Street, is the oldest operating wharf on the West Coast. It was built in 1872, when shipping was still the easiest way of transporting goods to and from Santa Barbara. Today the wharf functions mostly as a picturesque place to have fun—the buildings perch high above the water, the waves slap rhythmically against the pilings, while sea birds soar and cry overhead. A trip down to the wharf gives you a chance to see the city and the mountains from a novel perspective and take in the invigorating smell of the sea and the clean ocean breeze. On the wharf there are shops selling gifts and souvenirs, outdoor clothing, T-shirts, and ice cream, plus casual eateries, including one that specializes in fresh fish. The wharf is also where you'll find the Nature Conservancy and the Sea Center (reopening in 2004), with their intriguing educational facilities.

About a mile west of the wharf is the breakwater—a seawall that ends in a rocky, semicircular promontory—built to protect boats docked in the harbor. It is marked by the multicolored flags, representing twenty-six community service organizations, flying in the wind. A walk along this promenade on a windy day can be a wet and wild adventure! Six restaurants here offer menus ranging from very casual to fine dining.

While the wharf is mostly for fun, the breakwater is the business side of the marina and the place to go if you want sea gear, fishing supplies or advice, boating equipment, a cruise, a kayak, a beach chair,

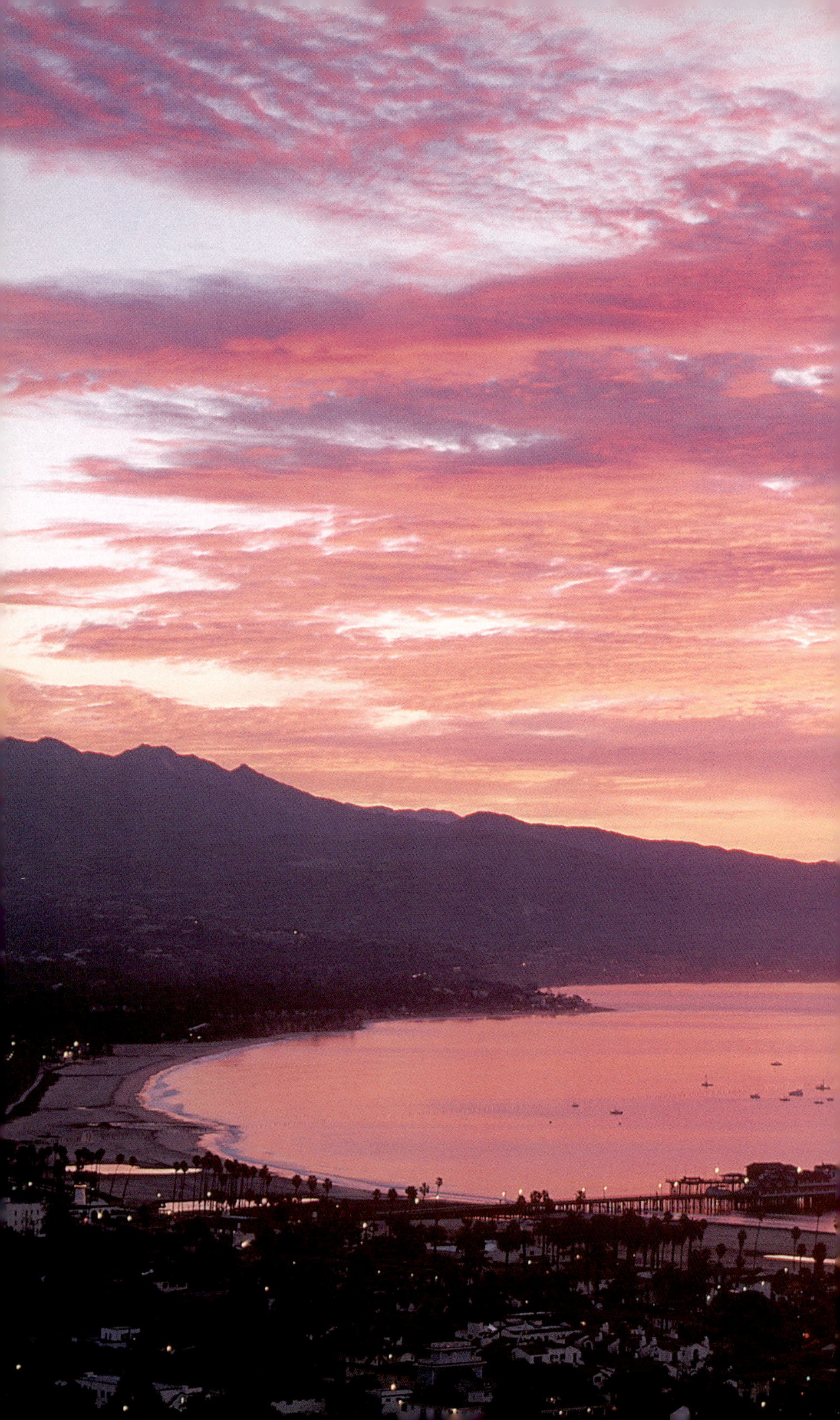

or a wet suit. Our harbor is home to over 1000 boats, and 70 of them are fishing vessels. To see the workings of the harbor get down there early. Morning for fishermen means sunrise—the brunch crowd misses the whole thing happening down at the dock. The fishing boats return in the afternoon to unload their catch.

    Like all of nature, the seaside is quieter at night. Try a nighttime stroll by the water to see the stars come out, watch the little ship lights glide by, and hear the waves lap steadily at the shore. Listening to the waves, you can almost hear them whispering, "Sleep well tonight, with the dawn begins another wonderful day in Santa Barbara."

Sunrise over Santa Barbara

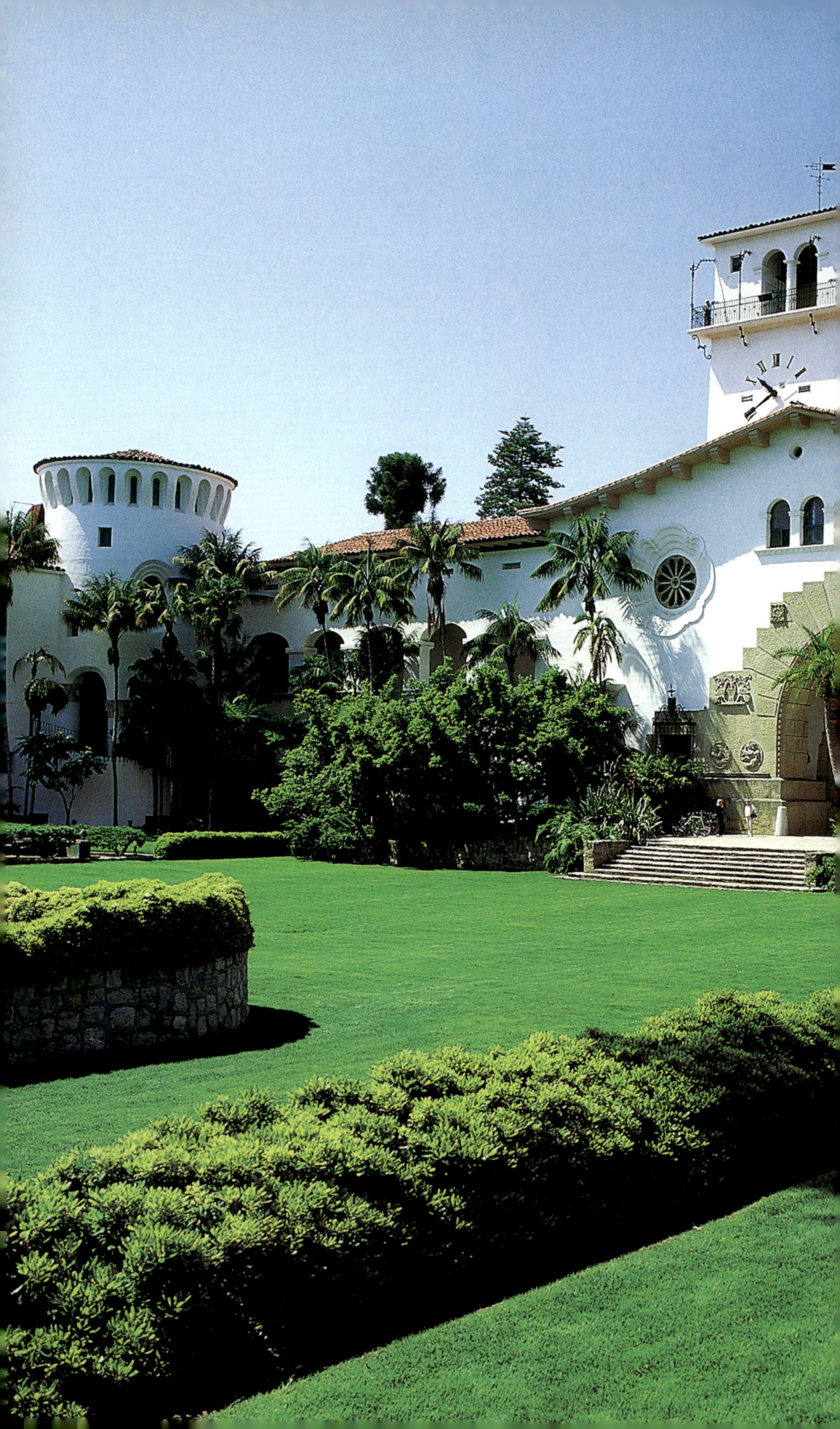

Art and Architecture
Chapter Three

Santa Barbara, to my mind, is art! A prime reason for Santa Barbara's wide reputation as a beautiful city is that artists, inspired by the fabulous natural garden around us, have had an influential hand in the city's creation. Above the entry of the architectural masterpiece that is the Santa Barbara County Courthouse, an inscription reads, "God hath given us the country, the skill of man hath built the town." These words are a perfect introduction to this art tour, which begins within sight of these words, in front of the County Courthouse, 1100 Anacapa Street.

The famous earthquake of 1925 ruined most of the buildings in Santa Barbara, including the old courthouse, built in 1873. The disaster, however, eventually proved to have a silver lining. Five years preceding that fateful earthquake, the city had established the Community Arts Association, with divisions dedicated to promoting music, arts, drama, plans and planting. Under the direc-

Courthouse Sunken Gardens

tion of Dr. Pearl Chase, to whom we are forever in debt, the Division of Plans and Planting became the catalyst for encouraging post-earthquake reconstruction of many Santa Barbara buildings in the Spanish Revival style. So when the new Courthouse was proposed, the city was re-embracing its Spanish cultural heritage. Completed in 1929, the Courthouse has magnificent design based on Spanish Revival architecture with an added Moorish twist. It became the gem of downtown, and, along with El Paseo, the inspiration for the city's new style.

Enter the Courthouse through the soaring sandstone arch facing Anacapa Street. The archway frames a majestic view of the grassy lawn, with pine and palm trees in the mid-distance and the mountains and sky beyond. The fountain to the left of the arch features a sandstone sculpture of a man and a woman, innocent but sensual.

By choice, Santa Barbara doesn't have many tall buildings; however, a trip to the Courthouse tower yields one of the rare views of our tierra adorada from on high. Reaching 85 feet above ground, the tower offers a breathtaking vista of the ocean to the south, the mountains to the north, a "red-tile view" of distinguished architecture in all four directions, plus a bird's-eye view of the garden below.

The Courthouse Sunken Garden, set among the destroyed foundations of the original courthouse, was planned as an informal botanical garden. It contains many rare and specimen plantings, identified in a brochure available at the docent's desk. I was married in this garden. For a farmer's daughter from the Midwest, to wed beneath the lavish, pink, saucer-shaped blossoms of Chinese magnolias in February(!) was a dream come true. Year around, the expanse of manicured grass is so beautiful that it is the chosen location not just for weddings but for many outdoor cultural events. Summer Solstice, the Fourth of July, and Fiesta, in August, all include public concerts on this lawn.

One of the most pleasing aspects of the Courthouse is its in-

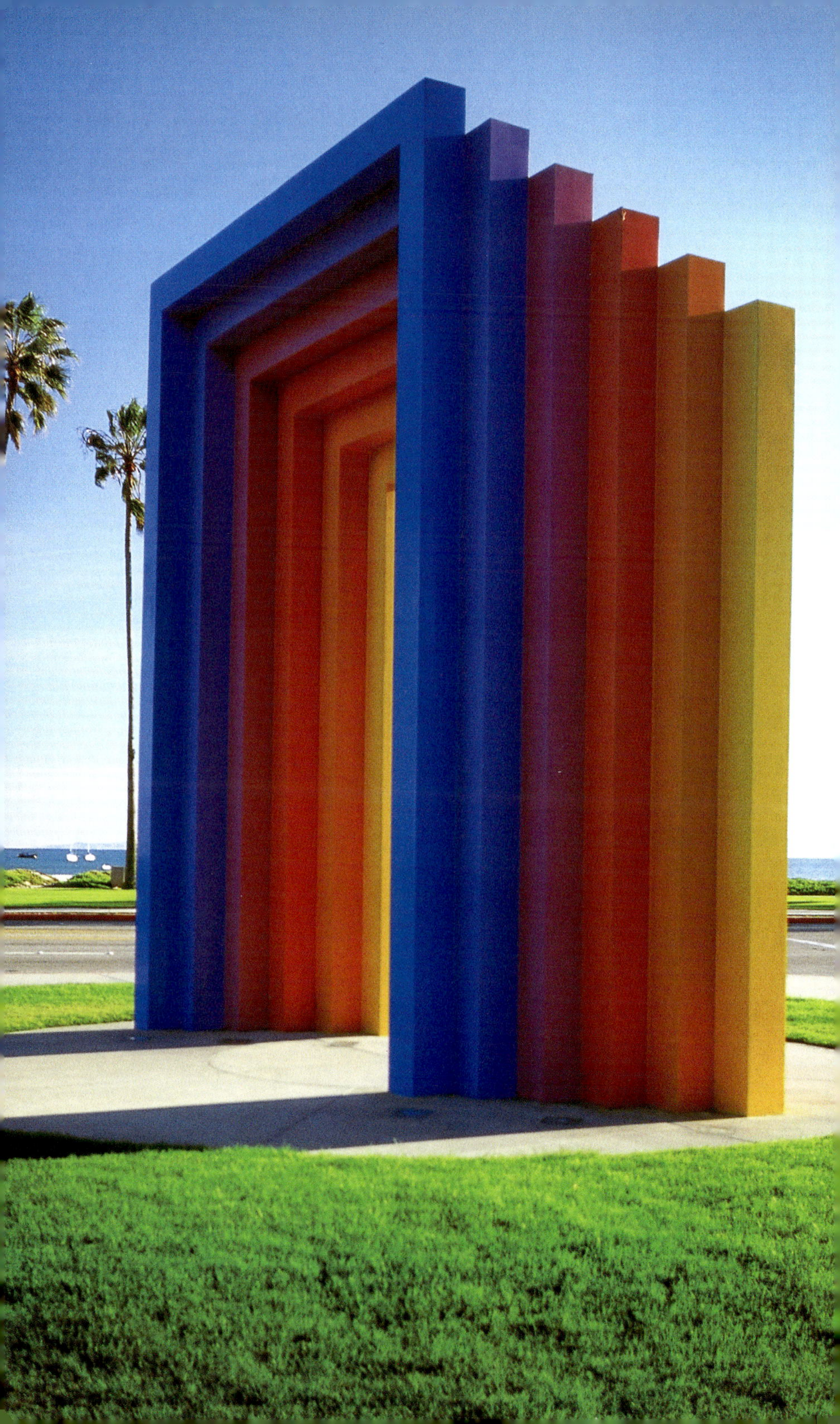

door-outdoor style, eminently appropriate for our Mediterranean climate. Open-air windows and exterior winding staircases enhance that indoor-outdoor feeling. Delicate ironwork finials, a mirador, balconies, and wrought-iron lanterns suggest the allure of a Spanish castle. Inside the Courthouse, you'll see Tunisian tiles, dramatic mosaic floors, and walls with romantic Spanish paintings and antiques that turn the corridors into galleries. On the second floor is one spectacular room whose walls are covered with murals depicting the settlement of Santa Barbara. The artist, Dan Sayre Groesbeck, worked for Cecil B. DeMille in Hollywood, and the influence of his days as a set-painter is evident in the flamboyant scenes painted here. Some say one of the figures looks like Errol Flynn. See if you can find him. Ask a docent to point out the former jail, now part of the Courthouse, and imagine how, even in jail, the prisoners of old had a small but poignant view of the paradise outside.

Our Courthouse is much loved and well cared for, as befits such an architectural treasure. The docents can show you wonders that you might not recognize on your own, as well as supply background information about Santa Barbara's history. Free docent-led tours begin at 2 P.M. Monday through Saturday, and at 10:30 A.M. Monday, Tuesday, and Friday.

The Art Museum

As you leave the Courthouse, walk along Anapamu (not Anacapa!) Street toward our next stop, the art museum. Along the way, you'll pass the public library at 40 E. Anapamu Street. Pause here to notice, above what was once the main entrance, an academic bas-relief. The brightly colored figures of Plato and Aristotle stand guard by the city's coat of arms, surrounded by the crests of four of the world's great libraries.

Continue down Anapamu to the Santa Barbara Museum of Art, at the corner of State and Anapamu Streets. Originally the city's post

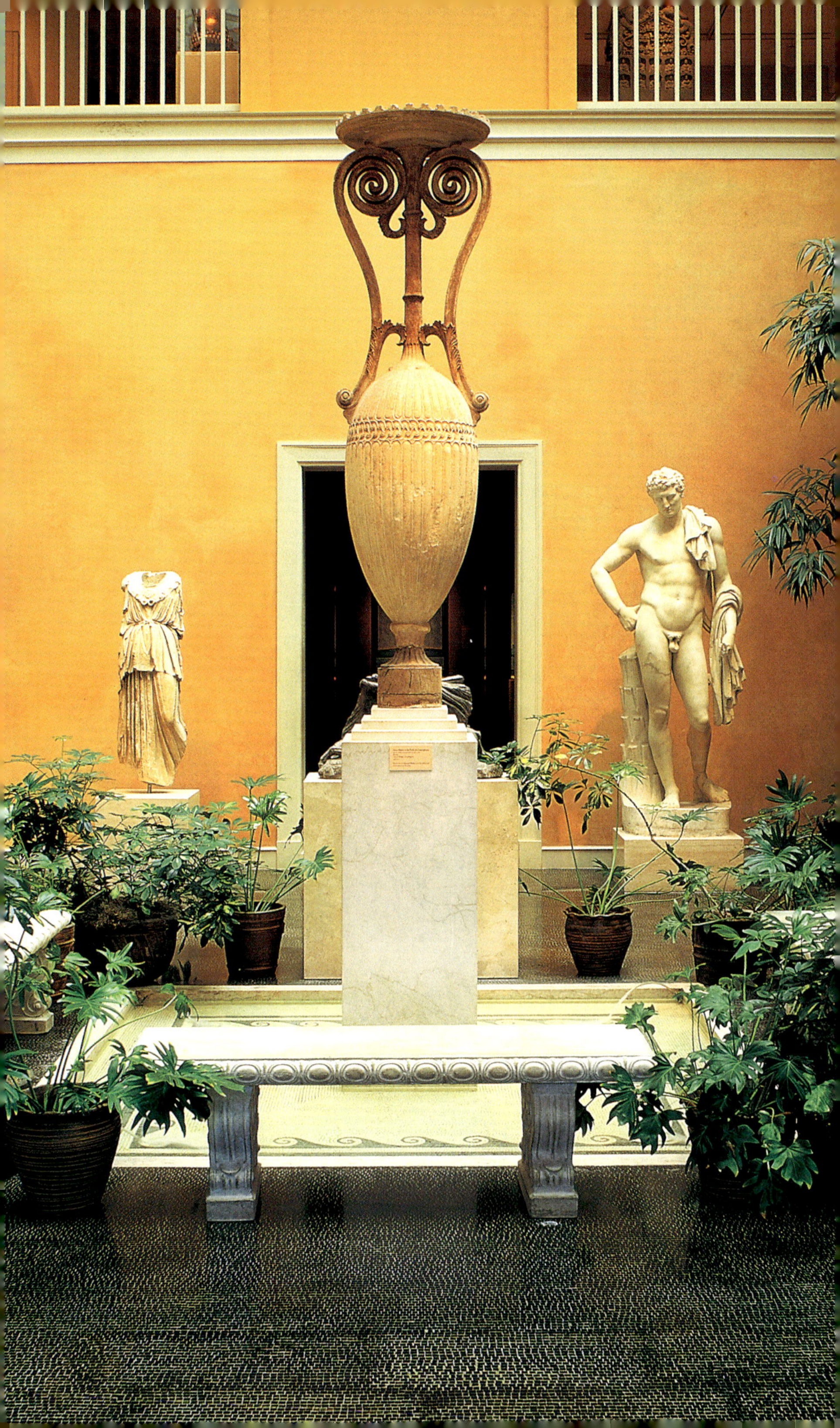

office, this classic building became our art museum in the 1930s. Characteristic of government offices, the original structure is set above the street on a plinth. As the museum's reputation and resources grew, it expanded into two more buildings to the south, gracefully adding the needed space while respecting architectural history.

Our art museum would be a jewel in a city of any size, but is particularly unexpected in a town as small as Santa Barbara. The museum has been favored by those with an attitude of *noblesse oblige*—the feeling on the part of the lucky in commerce to give back to the place where they live. The list of the museum's benefactors includes some of Santa Barbara and Montecito's noteworthy families. Just one example is the McCormick family, of spice fame, who gave the museum three magnificent Monets.

The Santa Barbara Museum of Art isn't the only recipient of so much generosity. Much of Santa Barbara today is the result of the vision and efforts of early arrivals who came for the climate and stayed on for the town. More often than not, they were educated, cultured people with inventive minds who had made their name and their fortune in the East. When they settled here, they put not just their money, but also their hard work, thoughtfulness, and creativity where their dreams were. Today, residents and visitors alike enjoy their gifts. Our hospital, wharf, Natural History Museum, Botanic Garden, Bird Refuge, zoo, schools, and theaters—the list goes on—all had fortunate beginnings thanks to big-hearted and progressive thinkers who had such affection for Santa Barbara.

Our museum continues to be funded by those who can afford to be so generous. Community participation at the museum is encouraged; for example, see the mural project involving talented local youth on the museum's back (east) wall. The museum has an imposing permanent collection and room for ever-changing temporary exhibits. The State Street entrance, framed by Greek columns, welcomes you through glass doors to the statuary garden named for one of the benefactors, Wright Ludington.

My favorite part of the art museum is the Asian gallery on the third floor. If you're coming just to look around for the first time and think you might enjoy seeing real samurai armor, or ancient and beautifully carved garden statues of goddesses and demigods, go there first. There are free docent-led tours every day at noon and at 1 P.M. The museum is open Tuesday through Saturday from 11 A.M. to 5 P.M., and Sunday from noon until 5 P.M. Friday nights it stays open until 9 P.M. It is closed Mondays and major holidays, and admission is free the first Sunday of every month. Another pleasant surprise here is the nice cafe and gift shop.

La Arcada

An art museum is a wonderful place to discover art. But since there are really no places where art cannot be found, keep your eyes wide open as you walk down the street—you're bound to see wonder in the unexpected nook. Let me mention a few spots to look for.

Walk out the art museum's back door through a freestanding arch and into the Library Arts Plaza. Here you'll find a sculpture titled "Intermezzo" by Anthony Caro. Then walk through La Arcada Court toward State Street, where you'll see Bud Bottoms' playful sculpture of dolphins. Don't miss the fountain full of real live turtles in front of the restaurant. Just before you reach the State Street sidewalk, mind that workman washing the windows! It's really a sculpture by J. Seward Johnson Jr., entitled "Nice to See You". Another of Johnson's pieces is located in the east wing of La Arcada Court bordering Figueroa Street—a life-size sculpture of an old gent on a bench sharing time with a child. An example of present-day citizen largesse, these works have been presented for the public to enjoy by Herb Peterson, owner of La Arcada, whose philanthropy has artfully enhanced uptown for many years. The lively fountains, flags, colorful plantings, and well-chosen sculptures and antiques he has provided make La Arcada a little bit of Europe in Santa Barbara.

La Arcada houses three intriguing art galleries that promote local art: the Waterhouse Gallery, the Bottoms Art Galleries, and Gallery 113. The culture of Santa Barbara attracts and produces matchless art, and many artists reside here. The area's innovative art community not only enhances our daily lives and encourages creativity but also promotes good will. For example, the local artists in the Oak Group work to protect not just the oaks but also the endangered undeveloped land and natural views in the Santa Barbara area. Like plein-air artists before them, they use their talents to raise public awareness and money for preservation, thereby safeguarding views for the artists to paint and the environment we live in.

Two locally owned businesses that should not be missed are right across Anapamu from the art museum. At Sullivan and Goss, Ltd. you'll find fine art books and wonderful plein-air and regional art. In the courtyard is an alfresco cafe. The Book Den, next door, is Santa Barbara's oldest used bookstore, selling new, used, and out-of-print books. You'll find the staff, all of them avid readers themselves, helpful and friendly.

The Arlington

North of the art museum on the west side of the street is the Arlington, more correctly, the Arlington Theater and Center for the Performing Arts. You can't miss its soaring spire. The theater was originally conceived as a gem in a chain of 1930s movie palaces. Two sumptuous hotels had preceded it on this spot. The first Arlington Hotel burned down in 1909; the New Arlington Hotel, built immediately after the fire, was a casualty of the 1925 earthquake.

The two hotels at this location, with their luxury accommodations, were pivotal in Santa Barbara's history—without them we would never have become a haven for the rich and famous. Through most of the 1800s, travelers arrived here via stagecoach, a dirty and unreliable journey. After Stearns Wharf was built in 1872, Santa Barbara became an easier destination for the traveler, and a trolley brought guests and their substantial luggage from the wharf to the Arlington Hotel. In 1901, the railroad finally closed the gap in the line that ran from San Francisco to Santa Barbara, and Santa Barbara-bound travelers could arrive on the most glamorous and comfortable transport of the times, the train. The second hotel was not rebuilt after the 1925 quake; instead, the beautiful and dramatic theater that we see now took shape.

This theater, designed by Joseph Plunkett, was the highlight of his career. Its distinguished tower rises above the surrounding structures, reminiscent of a cathedral from afar. If you are able, attend a live performance here, but even a movie seems glamorous when viewed at the Arlington. Fantasy balconies and stairways are painted along the walls, and stars twinkle in the ceiling—enter and you're transported to a nighttime setting in a Spanish village. Stroll into the outdoor lobby courtyard and look up at the walls just above the main lobby door to see the mural of whirling Spanish dancers. In fact, just standing outside the Arlington you can still catch the ambiance of early 1930s Santa Barbara. It's fun to imagine an event here in those days: the first automobiles pulling into the porte cochere, the beautiful people alighting to join the crowd in the tropical gardens. It is easy to believe that, during Prohibition, El Club Chico, a small private room behind the projector, served "the real thing".

Today, the colorfully tiled fountain, the ticket booth, and the rhythmic entry arches are as beautiful as ever. You can see a remnant of the hotel gardens if you look for the tree in front of 1309 State Street. This living vestige of the long-gone Arlington Hotel gardens, is a tall and graceful lyre-shaped silk oak (Grevilla robusta), with rust-colored blooms in spring. This venerable old tree has seen travelers come by steamboat, stagecoach, train, and finally by electric car to the grand hotels. When the first luxurious hotel burned down, the tree was singed. When the 60,000-gallon water reservoir (built to prevent another fire) on top of the second hotel collapsed in the catastrophic 1925 earthquake, the tree stood. As the early movie-goers arrived in their automobiles, it provided shade. It still graces State Street today.

The Arlington is the home of the Santa Barbara Symphony and is host to large touring musical and theater productions that visit here. The Granada Theatre, across the street, is one of the few buildings that survived the 1925 earthquake. Even though our population is nowhere near the size of our mega neighbor to the south, we often get the best in entertainment. Talented performers want to come here for the same reason that tourists do—everyone enjoys a day in Santa Barbara!

Across the street in the Arlington Plaza you might stop at the Delphine Gallery, 1324-D State Street, to view local art on display. (See the end of this chapter for information on a few compelling local art galleries not on this tour.) Meanwhile, it just might be time for a snack, or lunch, before making your way back down State Street. You'll find several restaurants on both sides of the street by the Arlington.

Don't overlook the opportunities for art afforded by the windows of retail establishments. Indigo, the Japanese furnishings store at 1323 State Street, is a rich example of how imaginative merchandising, which Santa Barbara does with such finesse, blurs the line between shopping and art. Several creative furniture/art/home decor dealers have opened in this area, invigorating the street with their energy. The abundance of artistic talent in residence in Santa Barbara makes living or visiting here all the more delightful—there's always a surprise (what will they think of next?).

As you stroll back down State approaching Sola Street, notice the unusual architectural style of the moderne building on the corner, the Christian Science Reading Room. This 1950s structure demonstrates how the city's architectural guidelines can be creatively modi-

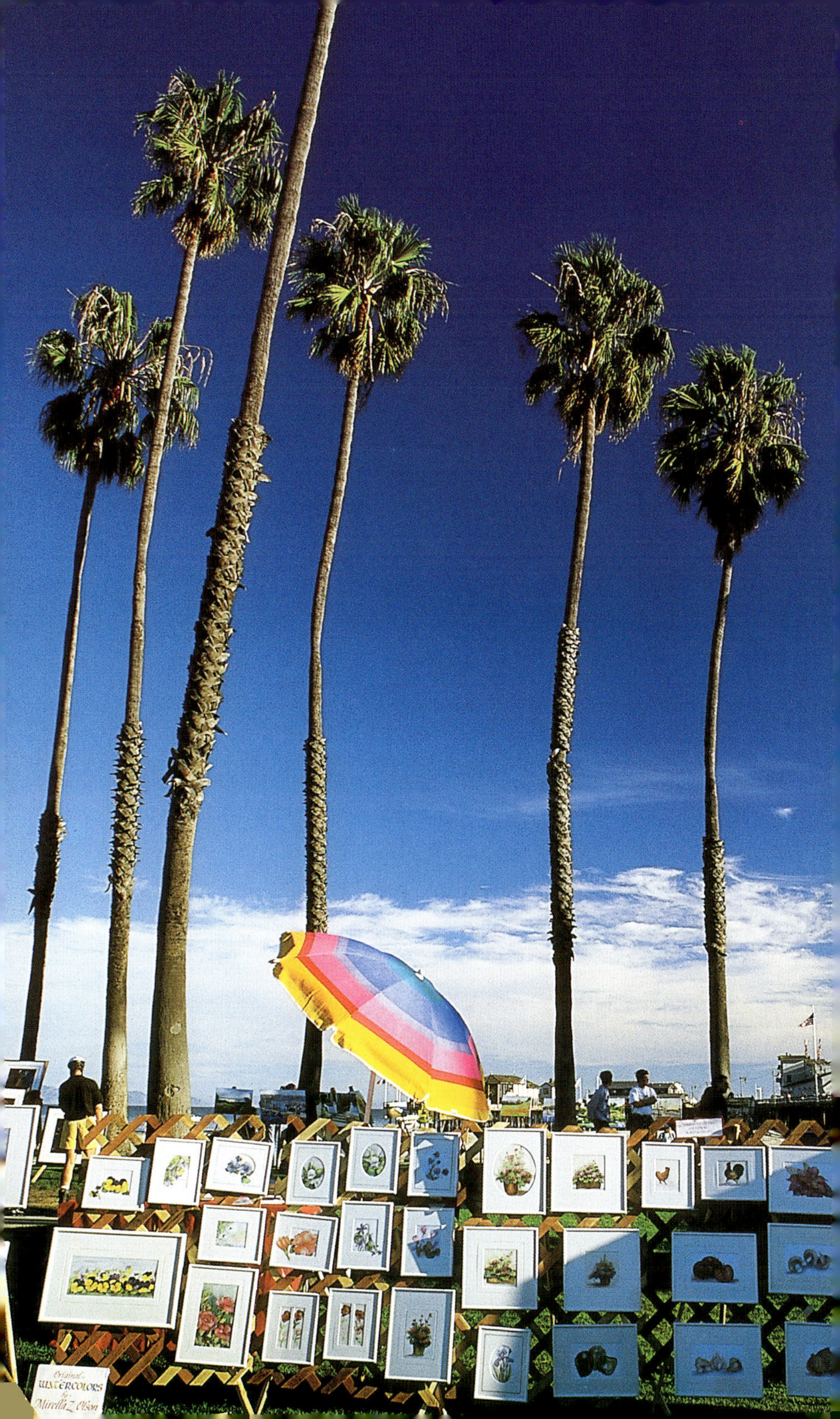
Original
WATERCOLORS
by
Mirella Z Olson

fied to encompass almost any kind of design. The building's curves and angles are peacefully married to the red-tile roofs and Hispanic style of the adjoining buildings.

When you reach Anapamu Street (across from the art museum), you might make a right turn and visit the Karpeles Museum, at 21 West Anapamu. History buffs in particular will enjoy this museum's collection of original letters, documents, and astonishing historical implements. This could be a once-in-a-lifetime chance to see the papers of George Washington, Einstein, and Napoleon. Elegantly housed and open to the public free of charge, this museum is another instance of civic generosity. It's open from 1 to 4 P.M. Wednesday through Sunday. If you're interested in photography, have a look next door at the newly opened Staton-Greenberg Gallery.

You might want to see how many different kinds of courtyards you can discover as you enjoy our city. Can you identify the magic blend of elements that makes these spaces seem so welcoming and private at the same time? For instance, continue a little farther down State Street until you find the address 1129 State. The dark entry opens into a beautiful courtyard that offers outdoor dining. Admire the detailed frieze around the entry and the top of the garden enclosure.

The next courtyard is a block away, at Aldo's, 1029 State Street. This restaurant, with offices upstairs, is built on the site of the Orella family adobe (circa 1857) and contains remnants of that old building within the walls. A tile commemorating the structure's historic status is on the exterior wall near the restaurant entrance. The Spanish Revival building you see now was built in 1927 as the Copper Coffee Pot Restaurant. Designed by the same architect as the Arlington Theater, it displays many of the same features, though in miniature. The tiny balcony, patio, fountain, and arcade are charming and visible from the street. Inside, you can see an original mid-nineteenth-century adobe wall and, from nearly a century later, one of the copper coffee

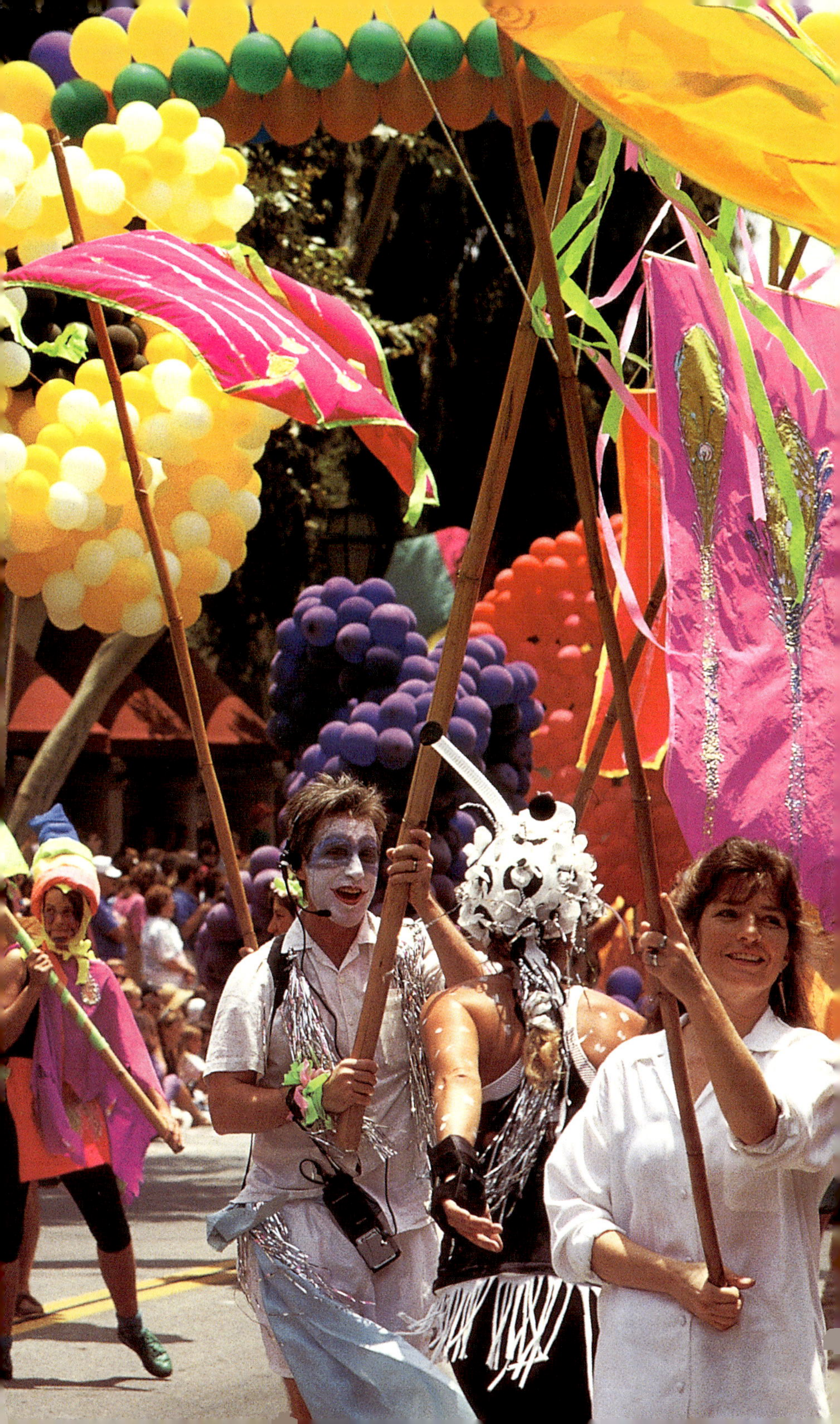

urns that kept the pulse of downtown going before the days of lattes and cappuccinos.

Recreation Center, Lobero Theatre, Post Office

Let's leave State Street for just a moment. Don't worry, we'll be right back. But first, continue on down State to the next corner, where State meets Carrillo Street. Turn left to follow Carrillo one block east to the corner of Anacapa Street, where you'll find a large brick building, the Carrillo Recreation Center. If you're a dancer, don't miss Friday and Saturday nights here in the ballroom, with a live band and excellent ballroom and swing dancers. The 87-year-old wooden floor is spring-loaded, providing shock absorption that makes all your steps a little livelier. The lessons offered before the dance will dust off your dancing shoes, and the small entry charge permits you to dance all evening in an atmosphere free of smoke and alcohol. On Sunday nights, the Santa Barbara Country Dance Society sponsors lessons and live music for folk and contra dancing. Call 897-2519 for dance information.

Next door to the south, at 924 Anacapa Street, is the Lobero Building, designed by Julia Morgan, the main architect for William Randolph Hearst's San Simeon Castle farther up the California coast. The Santa Barbara Chamber of Commerce and the Downtown Organization now have offices in this structure, originally built in the 1920s as a hotel for business women. What a perfect commission for a famous woman architect and an emancipated woman of her time! The lyrical stand of coral-colored bougainvillea gracing the façade, and the vents in the shape of peacocks on the upper floors, are wonderful feminine touches.

Speaking of architects, one of Santa Barbara's most renowned was George Washington Smith, who has to his credit the News-Press building on De la Guerra Plaza, the Little Town Club house on Carrillo Street, and many Santa Barbara and Montecito residences.

He, along with Lutah Maria Riggs, designed the stylish Lobero Theatre, built in 1924 on the corner of Santa Barbara and Canon Perdido Streets. This structure stands on what is the oldest theater site in California. The original building, an opera house, was constructed by Jose Lobero in 1873. The present building conveys an illusion of grandeur. Although it is only two stories high, its proportions glorify it; the theatergoer is humbled in comparison. Admire the handsome white columns at the front of the theater, and check at the box office for upcoming performances. Sometimes, even without advance planning, a few tickets can be had to a wonderful show. Small groups of jazz, rock, and classical musicians—including the popular "Sings Like Hell" music series—intimate drama, and dance are presented here. Inside, the theater is intimate yet elegant and comfortable, and almost every seat is a good one. (See chapter 1 for information on other performing arts theaters. For information on upcoming performances and the location of other small theaters, call 563-8068.)

Diagonally across from the Lobero Theatre, on Anacapa Street, you'll see the art deco steel-and-glass post office, at 836 Anacapa, built in 1937. Santa Barbara's movers and shakers were able to prevail upon the federal government to allow construction of this unusual design, in keeping with the style of the city, instead of the utilitarian boxes that were the prevalent design for post offices at the time. Right next to the post office is one of Santa Barbara's loveliest small courtyards, in front of the Presidio Plaza Building. This complex, at 802-812 Anacapa Street, was the final work of the famous architect Joseph Plunkett. Everything about this building, which contains an original adobe and parts of a 1906 hotel, exudes an air of the past. Notice the rooster weathervane atop the diminutive octagonal tower and dome. On the opposite side of Anacapa Street are the arches of the back entrance of handsome El Paseo. Our history tour of downtown started here.

Other Galleries

Before we conclude our little uptown art walk, I want to mention some innovative art spaces that are not on State Street. The Frameworks at 131 E. De la Guerra is just off State. The Channing Peake Gallery, 105 E. Anapamu, in the government building across from the Courthouse, is open Monday through Friday. The Marcia Burtt Studio, 517 Laguna Street, is open Wednesday through Sunday, from 1 to 5 P.M. A little farther away is the Living Green Gallery, a space devoted to sustainable and recyclable environment-friendly art. It's at 218 Helena Avenue, by the railroad tracks near the beach. Just outside Santa Barbara, in Montecito, is Easton Gallery, open weekends and by appointment; call 969-5781. Ms. Easton, long a champion of local artists, including some of the Oak Group painters, always shows high quality work.

To end our walk, go down De la Guerra Street to State Street, where you can't help but notice the entry to the colorful and exciting Paseo Nuevo, Santa Barbara's big outdoor international shopping mall. Passing through to the back (west side) of the mall, go upstairs to the Contemporary Arts Forum, one of the more provocative art spaces in town. They emphasize local art but might also have international or regional works, including the extra-visual.

After spending some time admiring art, I always begin noticing art everywhere. While you're still in that frame of mind, take a moment to enjoy the "double-distilled sweet idleness" on a bench or at a sidewalk table along State Street.

La Arcada
Barcliff & Bair
Cafe
SOCORRO
Casual Clothing
Natural Fabrics
OPEN

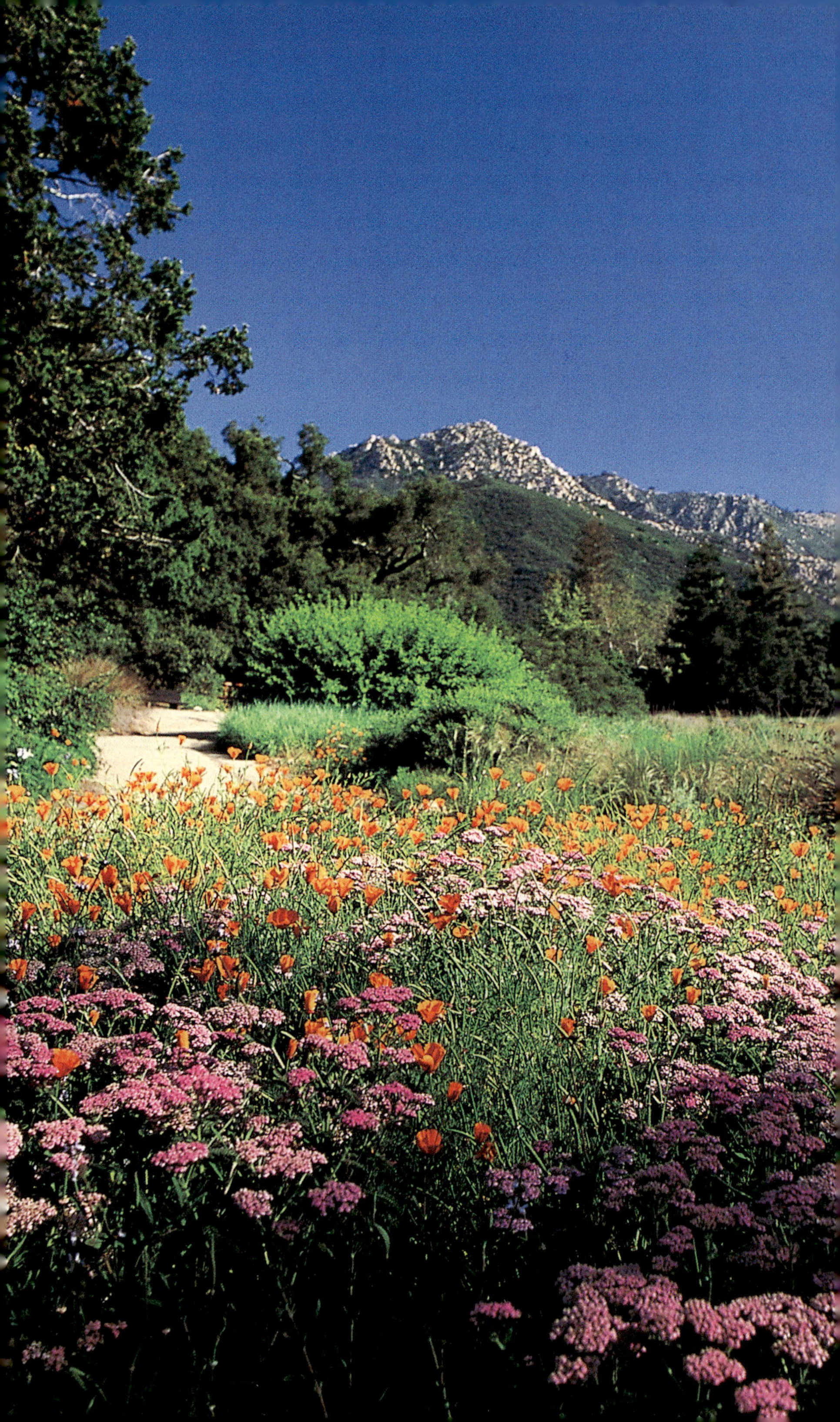

Parks and Gardens
Chapter Four

Paradise has no one description, but almost universally it is portrayed as a garden. One's first visual impression of Santa Barbara is just that: myriad shades of green foliage shot through with random brilliant color—the flowers. Plants discovered early on the formula for success: location, location, location. And our fortunate south-facing yet sheltered position on the coast makes Santa Barbara a horticultural Eden. Residents, forgetting that many plants that luxuriate here are exotic and unexpected, chuckle to see tourists from around the world taking videos and pictures of seemingly every vine and tree. Those who have gardened elsewhere attest to the fact that growing things in Santa Barbara requires comparatively little effort. The instructions at any time of year around here are shamelessly easy: plant it, keep it moist, and most likely it will grow.

The extraordinary number of species that can flourish in Santa Barbara includes

Botanic Gardens

plants that prefer the jungle, but our climate is much more temperate. Succulents are perfectly suited for our landscape, yet ferns do well here, too. And although roses and lemons are cultivated commercially, we are famous for our orchids. The secret life of the plants that usually prefer more tropical conditions is that they make ingenious use of our summer fog. The morning fog deposits prism-like drops of moisture on leaves. When the sunshine begins to break through the haze, the plants use those drops of water like a magnifying glass to intensify the photosynthesizing effects of the sun. Usually by noon, the sun is shining brightly and you'd never know we'd had a cool, foggy morning, yet the exotic coral tree outside the door is thriving as if it's in Brazil.

The real sport is to find out what *doesn't* grow in Santa Barbara. As the first resident plant lovers discovered the propensity for flora to thrive here, they engaged in this sport in their garden plots. Madame Walska comes immediately to mind. Her Montecito estate, named Lotusland, with its exotic and bizarre plants, beguiles to this day. She convinced her traveling friends to play courier for her, securing plants from every part of the world for her garden. The Italian horticulturalist Francesco Franceschi is another, a landscape designer in the largest sense of the word. His late-nighteenth-century nursery on the Riviera has become Franceschi Park, at 1510 Mission Ridge Road, with panoramic views as beautiful today as they were a hundred years ago. His love of horticultural experimentation effected a lasting change in our surroundings because some of his specimens grew, thrived, and reproduced.

He was not alone. Both amateur and trained botanists planted their desires in the form of pips and saplings, and many of them flourished. Those informal gifts give Santa Barbara the look of a casual botanic garden to those interested in the possibilities of seed. Since the earliest gardeners in this area were all transplants themselves, they must have been amazed to discover that almost everything could thrive here. What a delight when they found that some of those experiments were wild successes!

One example, from 1872, is a magnificent single grapevine in Montecito that sprawled over an acre of land, producing an annual average yield of 14,000 pounds of grapes. This extraordinary plant was sent to the Centennial Exposition in Philadelphia in 1875, where it became a main attraction. If you want to see with your own eyes what our soil, the sun, and ocean breezes can encourage, take a look at our famous Moreton Bay fig tree, a transplant from its native Australia. The fig, a gift from a sailor, is over 130 years old and could shade the residents of a small town! The largest tree of its kind in the United States, it's located at Chapala and Montecito Streets near the railroad depot. With such extraordinary results from some of the early experiments, it's not surprising that agriculture is still one of Santa Barbara County's most important industries. We grow flowers, strawberries, broccoli, and wine grapes for the world.

Farmer's Markets

One of the most sensual rewards of being in Santa Barbara is the number of fruits, flowers, and vegetables available every day. The gifts of nature are at our fingertips because farmer's markets enable us to buy fresh-picked produce directly from our local growers. There are farmer's markets every day except Sunday, with the largest one on Saturday morning, from 8:30 A.M. to 12:30 P.M., downtown at Cota and Santa Barbara Streets. Shopping the market is a beautiful, tasty, and healthful experience. It's also an agricultural lesson to see the staggering variety of tropical and subtropical produce changing with the season. And it's fun. You'll be entertained by musicians, and sometimes magicians, as you wander the colorful stalls and talk to the growers. Smaller farmer's markets are held at State and Cota Streets on Tuesday afternoons from 3:30 to 6:30, in La Cumbre Plaza on Wednesdays, in Goleta on Thursdays in the Calle Real Shopping

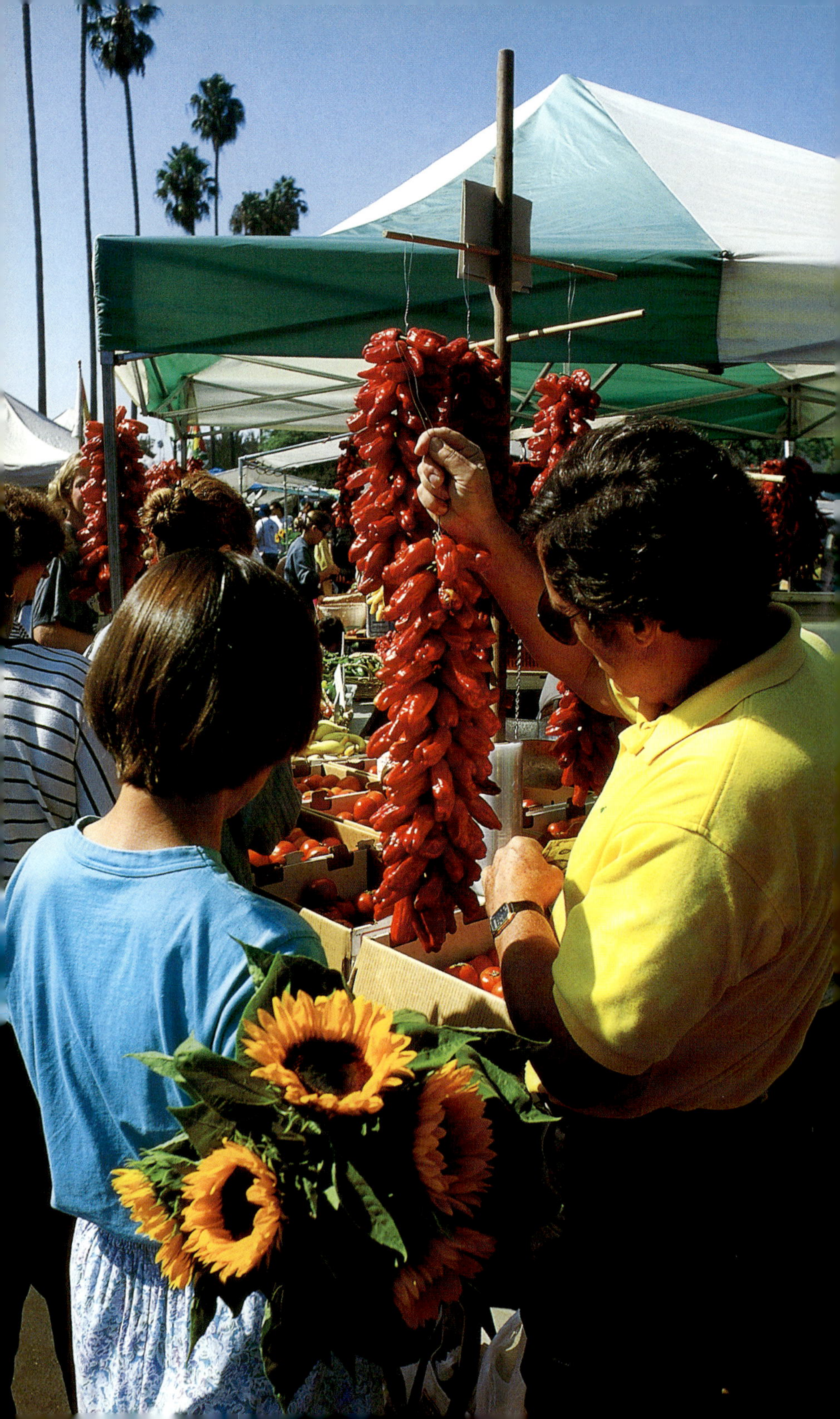

Center from 3 to 6 P.M., and in Montecito on Friday mornings, 8:30 A.M. to 11 A.M. For information about the farmer's markets, call 962-5354.

Fairview Gardens Farms in Goleta has organic produce for sale at a roadside stand at 598 N. Fairview Avenue. The stand is right at the edge of their prolific organic farm, where they use the most progressive "green" methods. Another produce stand in Goleta is Lane Farms Green Stand at 308 Walnut. Tri-County Produce at 335 S. Milpas by the beach, although not a "farmer's" market, has been locally owned for two generations and offers a vast selection of fresh produce seven days a week. At any of these locations you'll see extensive displays of nature's bounty—awesome and appreciated.

Gardens for Walking

The beautiful land in and around Santa Barbara provides another kind of treat for the senses: walking through nature. This ramble can be either an urban or a wilderness affair. The "Garden City," as Santa Barbara has been called, has more than enough gardens to keep the amateur botanist or beauty-lover busy for several seasons. Some of the following are not-to-be-missed showplaces; others are more like cultivated whimsy or tranquil resting spots.

The Botanic Garden

One of the nicest places to walk in Santa Barbara is the Botanic Garden, 1212 Mission Canyon Road. Established in 1926 as Anna Blaksley-Bliss's memorial to her father, the garden was used to research and display plants native to the Pacific slope of the United States. It covers more than 65 acres and has 5 1/2 miles of scenic trails. Along these trails you can pass through meadows, canyons, redwood stands, oak groves, and Mission Creek. The garden also has a library, a home demonstration garden, and a tea house. Its plantings are mostly native, and something is in bloom every month of the year. Spring is especially spectacular in the Santa Barbara foothills because of the profusion of orange California poppies and the purple lupine. Why not experience a mini version of this wonder at the Botanic Garden? My friend Cassie says you can enjoy "heaven on earth" if you take a sandwich up to the picnic area in the meadow on a spring day when the poppies are in bloom. Not only does our unusual climate allow a wide variety of plants to thrive, there is rarely a fly or mosquito to hamper our enjoyment of the outdoors! In this native garden, you can enjoy the sweeping chaparral vistas you would see otherwise only from a high trail in the foothills. Or try to identify as many of the 1000 species of rare and indigenous California plants growing here as you can. Flowers with names like Indian paintbrush, blue-eyed grass, shooting star, and chocolate lily await your visit. Enjoy!

City Parks

Just at the edge of downtown is Alice Keck Park Memorial Gardens, covering a complete city block at 1500 Santa Barbara Street. This lovely park features a pond with koi and water lilies, several types of gardens, benches, winding paths, a sundial, and best of all, I think, a directory so you can find the proper name of any plant you are admiring. Almost every kind of tree and bush you'll see in Santa Barbara is planted here—a living kaleidoscope of shapes and color for all seasons.

Across the street, at Alameda Park, lovely palms grace the soft green grass for an afternoon of reading on a blanket. There are picnic benches for a midday snack or an all-afternoon barbecue. Here, too, is Kid's World, its beckoning colorful playground equipment covered with happy youngsters. If you haven't felt like a kid for quite a while, why not stop, watch, and take a lesson?

There are neighborhood parks in every part of town. For information about any city park, its location and facilities, regulations, hours, and related topics, see the website: www.sbparksandrecreation.com.

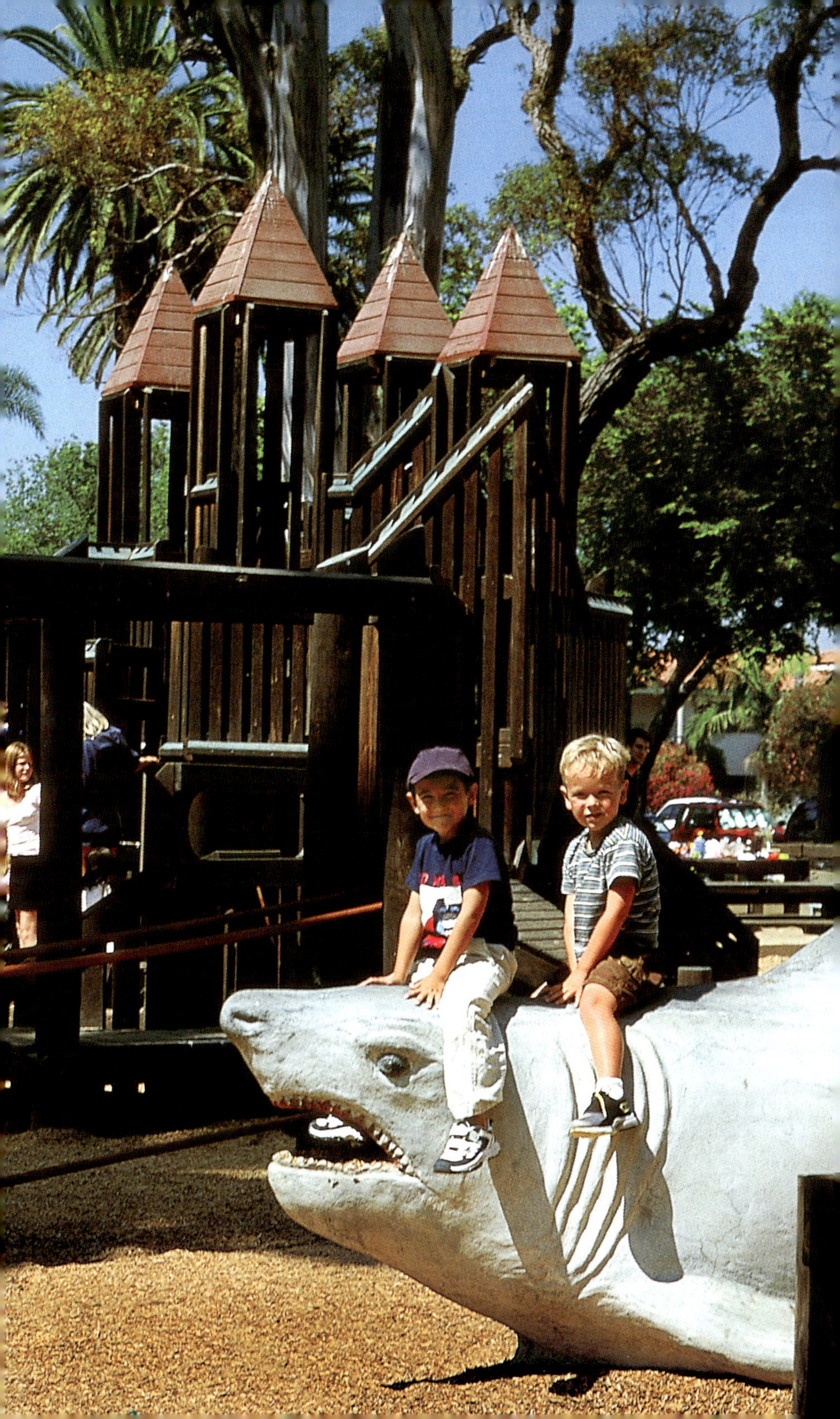

Dogs are not allowed off leash in any city park except one. If "park" for you means a place where your dog can run, check out the Douglas Family Preserve-and don't forget your poop scoop. The preserve, located on the mesa at the end of Medcliff Road and Selrose Lane, was rescued from development by the people of Santa Barbara, with the generosity of the Kirk and Michael Douglas family. It overlooks the ocean above Hendry's Beach.

If you'd like to view specimen trees of solemn beauty, walk the blocks of East Anapamu Street through the Italian Stone Pine Allée. This arched passage of majestic trees, a long-ago gift from Francesco Franceschi, extends for five city blocks, starting at 300 East Anapamu and ending near Milpas Street. If you continue along Milpas, you'll get a glimpse of the Santa Barbara Bowl, 1122 N. Milpas, which hosts fabulous outdoor concerts, often under the stars. This small outdoor venue, one of the finest in the country, was built as a WPA project in 1936.

During the summer, a great place to hear a free outdoor concert is Chase Palm Park, 236 East Cabrillo Boulevard, right across from the beach. The summer series of free concerts mostly feature popular local musicians, and all genres of music. Check the upcoming schedule at 564-5418 or www.sbparksandrecreation.com. This series has become a wonderful community get-together. It is especially great for families with kids who might not be ready for the stage but can definitely enjoy music and a crowd on the grass. Bring your picnic and a blanket, and be ready to park several blocks away due to the event's popularity.

Botanical Demonstration Garden

At Santa Barbara City College, located on the bluffs above the harbor, are magnificent views of the coastline near Ledbetter Beach. You can visit the Chumash Ethnobotanical Preserve native garden on campus, and also the Lifescape Garden, a collection of over 700

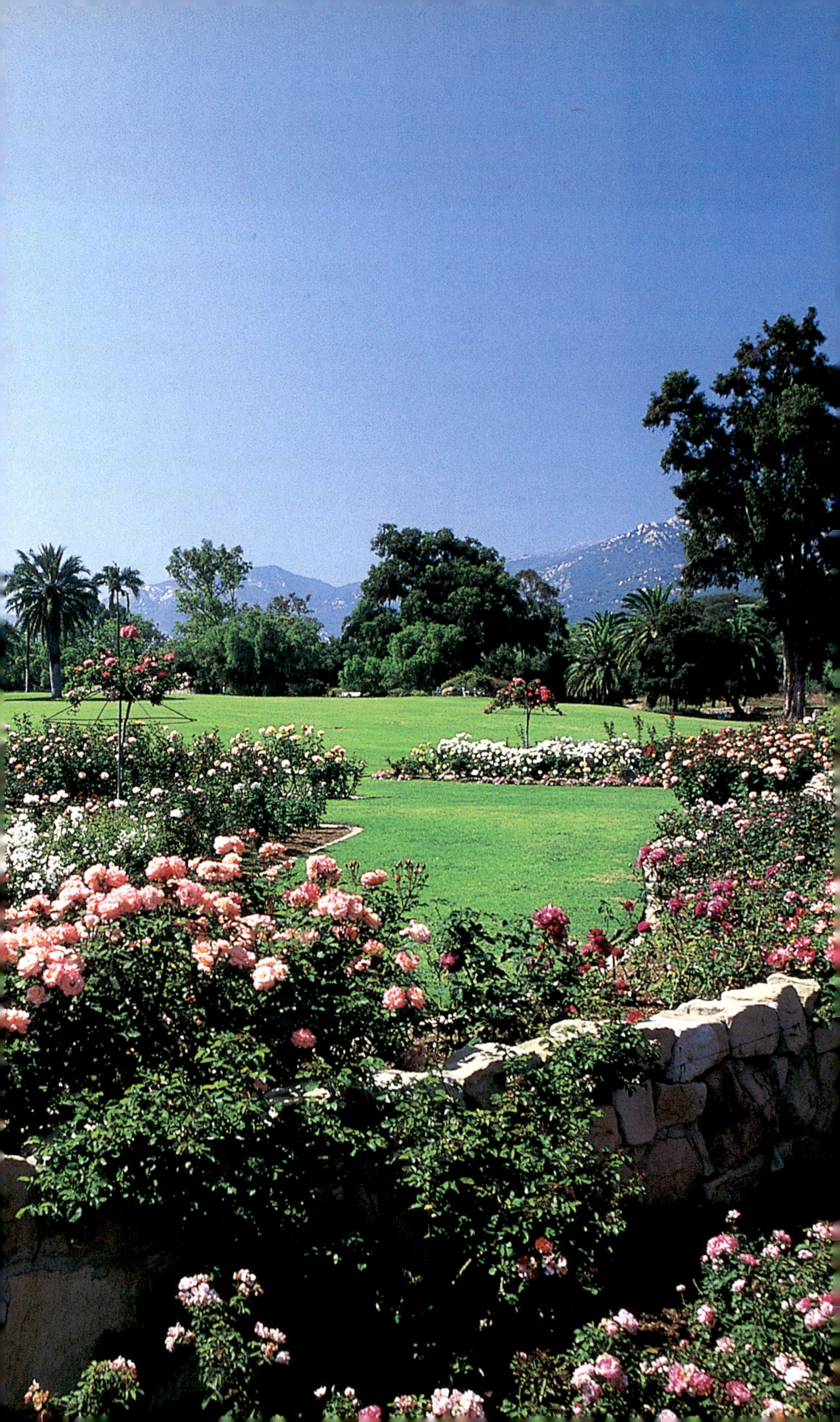

edible and ornamental plants that includes displays of many "green" garden practices. The City College garden is located at 721 Cliff Drive. If you'd like to visit a drought-tolerant garden in bloom, look in on the one outside the Goleta Valley Water District offices, just north of the Santa Barbara city limits at 4699 Hollister Avenue.

Montecito Estates

There are gardens and then there's Lotusland, the legendary garden in Montecito. Ganna Walska, a Polish opera singer born in 1887, cultivated rich men who became her husbands. After buying her estate in Montecito, she spared nothing to create one of the most startling horticultural sites I've seen. Yes, it has a lotus pond. It also has extremely rare cycads and a euphorbia garden that is just plain kinky. In addition, there are topiaries, pools, lawns, orchards, and color gardens. The plantings became the backdrop for a powerful and original woman who took everything to the limit. Lotusland is a philosophy as much as a garden. Not a spur-of-the-moment place to visit, it's worth the trouble to get a reservation for a tour. Call 969-9990 months in advance of the time you'd like to visit.

San Francisco columnist Herb Caen once described Santa Barbara as "having an overabundance of bougainvillea and the delectable smell of old money." I feel he was aptly describing Montecito, the small community that borders Santa Barbara to the south. Since Montecitans value their privacy, mostly what one sees in residential areas is the bougainvillea spilling over the gate or the giant green shrubbery that secludes the occupants and their gardens. But to see beyond the gates of one prime estate, visit the 75-year-old mansion and 11-acre grounds of Casa del Herrero. The house was designed by George Washington Smith, and the gardens were planned by Lockwood de Forest and Ralph Stevens—the premier designers of their day. The 90-minute guided tour through this well-maintained estate is made fascinating by the articulate docents and is well worth

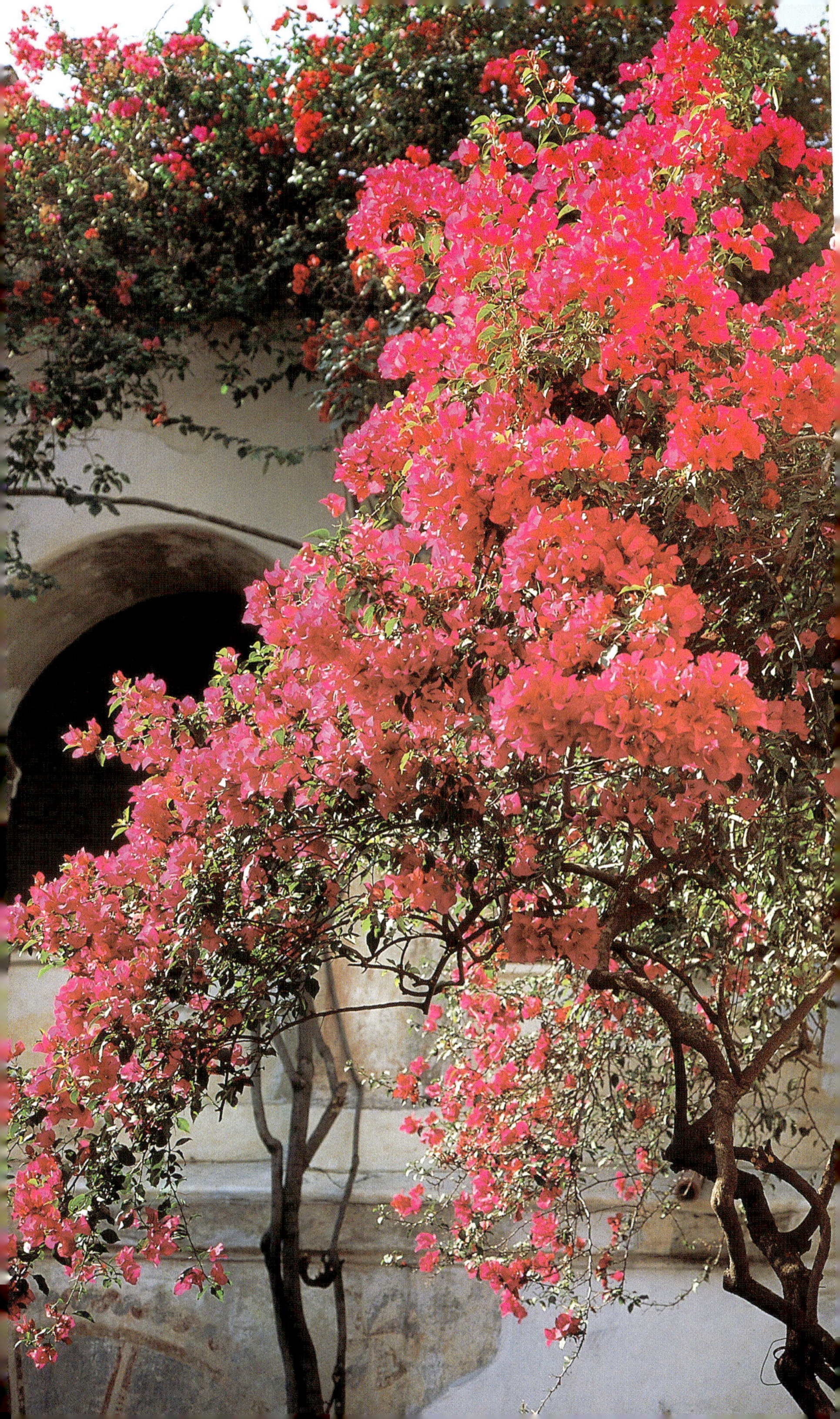

the $15 admission. A place on a Wednesday or Saturday tour can be reserved by calling 565-5653 (preferably a month in advance.)

The Flowers

For a stunning array of seasonal floral color, let your eyes take in the zillions of cut flowers available at the various farmer's markets. Some growers will allow you to visit their fields and greenhouses, mostly located in outlying Carpinteria and Goleta. Flower lovers will think they've died and gone to heaven when they visit either the Santa Barbara Orchid Estate, located at 1250 Orchid Drive in Goleta, or Gallup and Stribling Orchid Visitor Center in Carpinteria at 3450 Via Real. Riding a bicycle around either of these orchid estates, you will get glimpses of other neighboring orchid growers as well as seeing the many different types of flowers Santa Barbara grows commercially, for example, Gerbera daisies and roses. Santa Barbara's annual orchid show, usually held in February at the Earl Warren Showgrounds, draws people from all over the world who appreciate or covet these exotic blooms.

The Festivals

Judging by the weekends, Santa Barbara seems to be in a constant state of celebration. And what could be a nicer setting for a celebration than a garden or a park? The largest local festivities often have their finale in the Courthouse Sunken Garden. The several ethnic festivals, which draw bigger and bigger crowds every year, are held in Oak Park at 300 W. Alamar Avenue. Tourists might otherwise never see this park, but it is worth a visit even if there is no entertainment. Under the shady oak trees that give the park its name are picnic tables and barbecue pits. Beyond the wooden bridge is a dance platform for full-moon prancing that also serves as a stage for entertainers during the festivals. These cultural events-cum-outdoor parties serve up ethnic food, with all-day entertainment that ranges

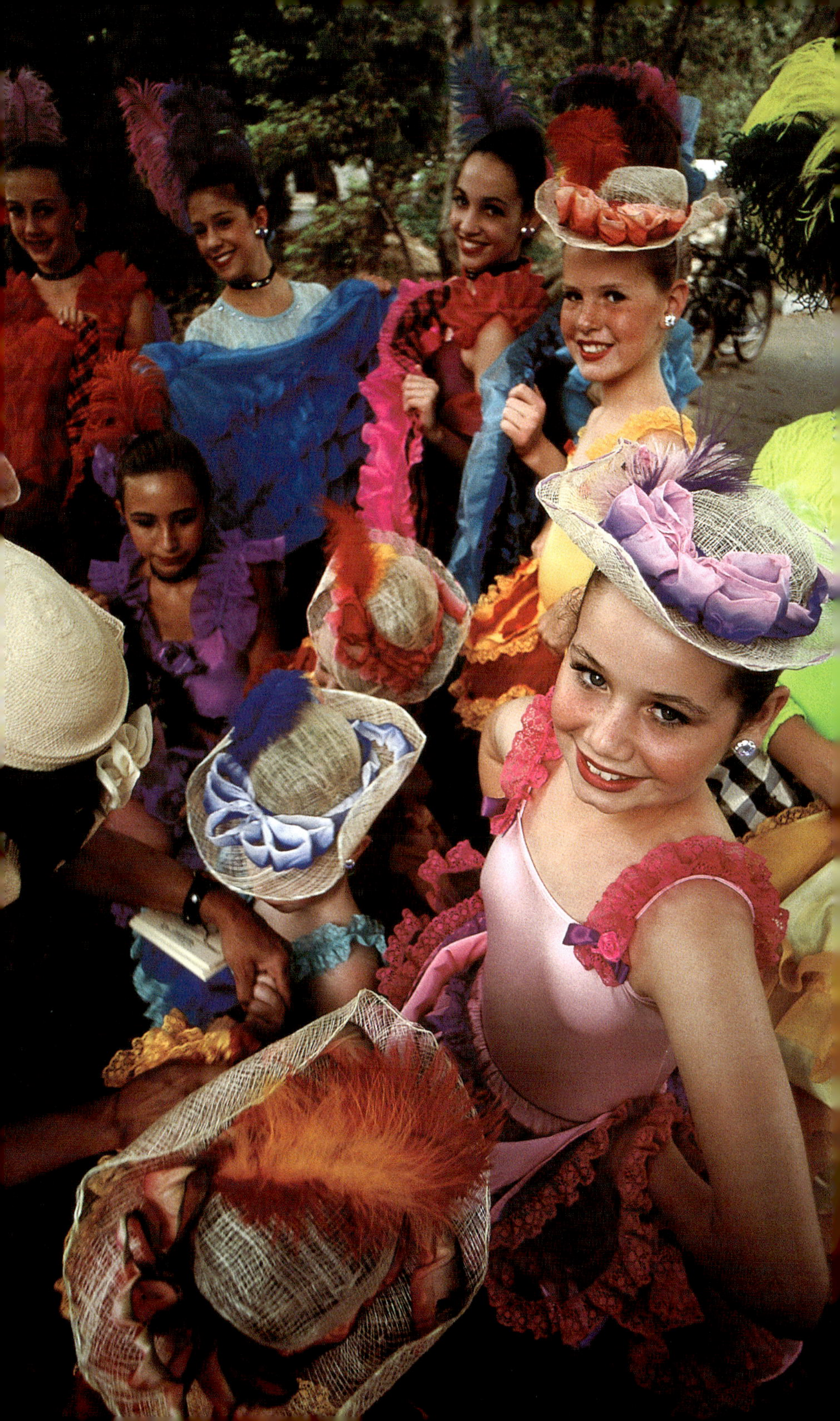

from Irish dancing to French Poodle contests, depending on the date. (See the calendar of events at the back of the book for approximate dates of these festivals.)

Hiking

It's exceptional to find so many well-maintained trails leading to such glorious sights immediately outside a city, and thanks in part to the cooperation of numerous community organizations, there's a trail in the Santa Barbara foothills suitable for everyone. Some are rugged and challenging; others are appropriate for families with children and are enjoyable for people who don't ordinarily include physical effort in their definition of relaxation.

If "hiker" doesn't usually describe you, or if you're on your own, don't let that stop you from stepping out in Santa Barbara. There are several two-or-three-hour urban hikes one can enjoy, or check the Independent newspaper (free, delivered Thursdays) to see what the Sierra Club has planned. The club has free guided hikes on Saturday and Sunday mornings, usually meeting at 9 A.M. in the Bank of America parking lot, at the corner of State and Hope. The club also organizes strenuous hikes on Wednesday evenings that meet at 6:30 P.M. at the Old Mission—bring a flashlight and water—and a social hike on Friday night that meets at 6 P.M. at the Old Mission. The Sierra Club schedule in the Independent (under weekly events, Saturday and Sunday) suggests the level of fitness for each hike and provides a phone number for further information. The leaders are experienced hikers, and after sign-up, the group often carpools to the trail head.

There are also good, informative books that give instructions for some of the one hundred hikes in the area that start just minutes from the beach or the Mission. My favorite is *Walk Santa Barbara* by Cheri Rae and John McKinney.

Every mid-October, the monarch butterflies arrive to stay through the winter until February, relaxing in the eucalyptus groves just north of Santa Barbara, past Goleta. Their ability to migrate in such great numbers, and to find the same groves year after year, is miraculous. To witness this awe-inspiring natural wonder first-hand, take 101 north to the Storke Road/Glen Annie exit, and after getting off the freeway, turn left, toward the ocean. Continue to the first stoplight, and there make a right onto Hollister Avenue. Drive on Hollister 1.4 miles, until you see a white wall on the left side of the road that says "Santa Barbara Shores." Turn left at Santa Barbara Shores Drive, and continue .3 miles to the road's dead end. Park (on a residential street) and enter the fenced-in monarch grove area. Follow the dirt path about 50 yards, where it leads into the eucalyptus trees to the left. The signs there will guide you.

The butterflies are resting from their migration, and they cling to the leaves of the eucalyptus trees, mostly in the higher branches. As the day warms above 55 F., they begin to fly about. Spotting them can be frustrating if you don't know what you're looking for, because their closed wings look very much like the leaves. But if you are quiet and patient as you look toward the sky, you will be rewarded with the sight of many—maybe hundreds or thousands—of monarchs, occasionally beating their wings as they drowse. You may see the restless ones leave and take flight for a fluttering short glide through the surrounding treetops. Later, after watching the butterflies, you might enjoy continuing your hike to the nearby estuary to see local birds.

A special treat during winter and spring is the refreshing sight and sound of Mission Creek flowing among the boulders in Rocky Nook Park, at 610 Mission Canyon Road, just a short walk from the Mission. The park, which offers plenty of shade trees and picnic tables, also boasts the county's oldest bridge, lovingly crafted from stone. Rocky Nook Park is just one of the 28 Santa Barbara County parks. For information about any county park, visit their website: www.sbparks.org. All city and county parks are open from sunrise to dusk, and require dogs to be on leash.

Wherever you find yourself in Santa Barbara, take a moment to appreciate and enjoy the garden all around you!

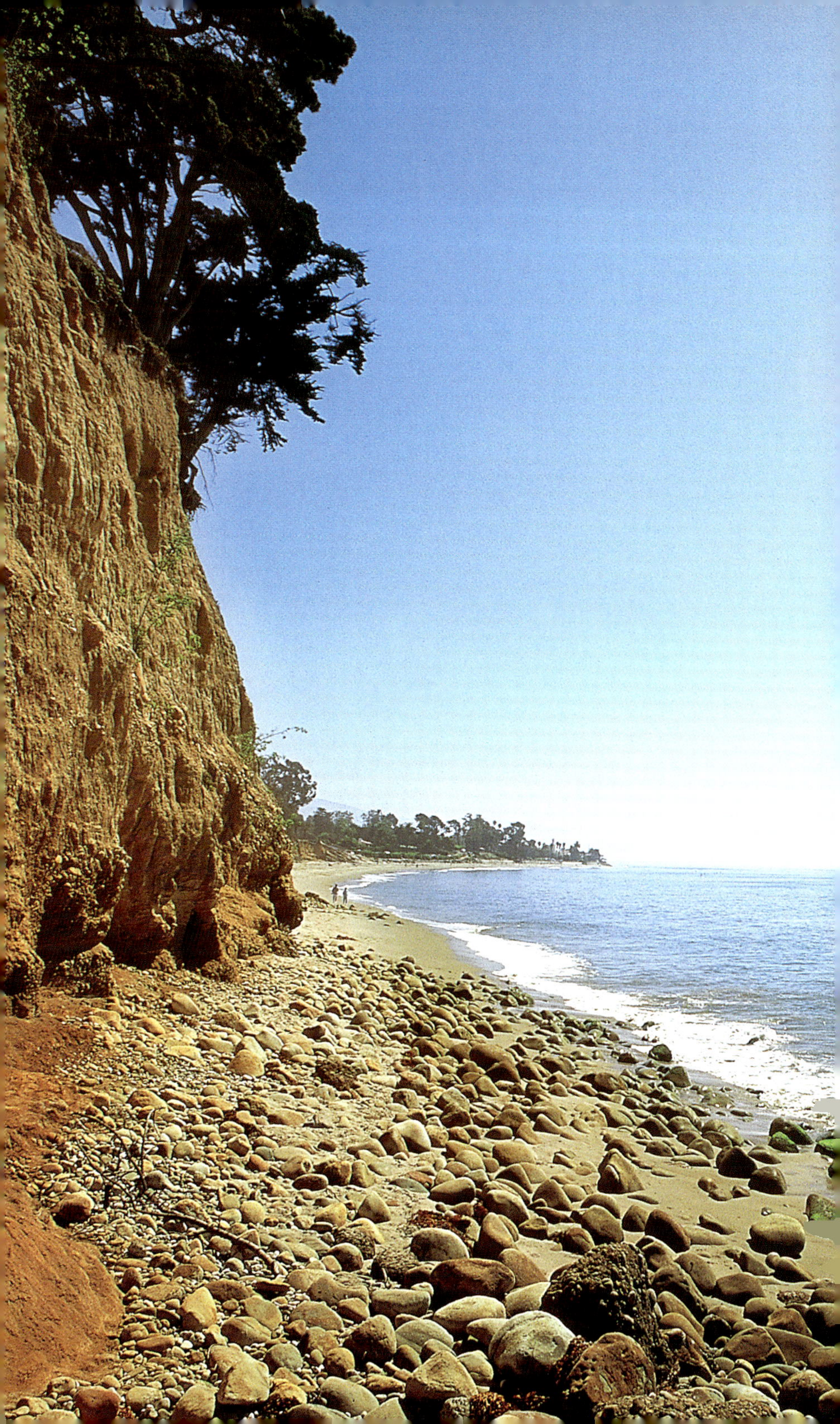

Best Places in Santa Barbara

Some travel to find themselves, some travel to forget; in either case, there are certain experiences that the traveler hopes to encounter. Here are some Santa Barbara experiences that come with local recommendations. What makes something a "best place" is subjective and may change, but at this moment the following are some of the best places in Santa Barbara to find:

A Map
The Visitor Center kiosk at the beach, on the corner of E. Cabrillo Blvd. and Garden St. (walk-in only). They can also help with last-minute weekday lodging, 965-3021.

A Strong Cup of Coffee Downtown
Coffee Cat, 1201 Anacapa (across from Courthouse); **Cafe Sienna**, 1101 State St.

Bicycle Maps and Info
www.trafficsolutions.info, or 963-save
Santa Barbara Bicycle Coalition, www.sbbike.org.

Sunrise
The harbor

Sunset
The Biltmore Beach, along Channel Drive
Shoreline Park, at Shoreline Drive and La Marina

An Inexpensive Breakfast
The Minnow at the breakwater
Cajun Kitchen, 901 Chapala St. (downtown) or 1924 De la Vina St.

Souvenirs Downtown
Enlightened Sights, 819 State St.

Accommodations (in Advance) for the Weekend
Santa Barbara Hot Spots, 36 State St., (800) 793-7666

Best Idea for Enjoying Your Vacation in Santa Barbara:
Park your car; Santa Barbara is a pedestrian's paradise. www.Santabarbaracarfree.org, 696-1100

The City's Top 10 Highlights for $2 (Round trip)
Via the eco-friendly electric shuttle, from the waterfront to the Mission. Ask about the Field Trip, 683-3702, which runs from Memorial Day through Labor Day.

Bluffs at Butterfly Beach

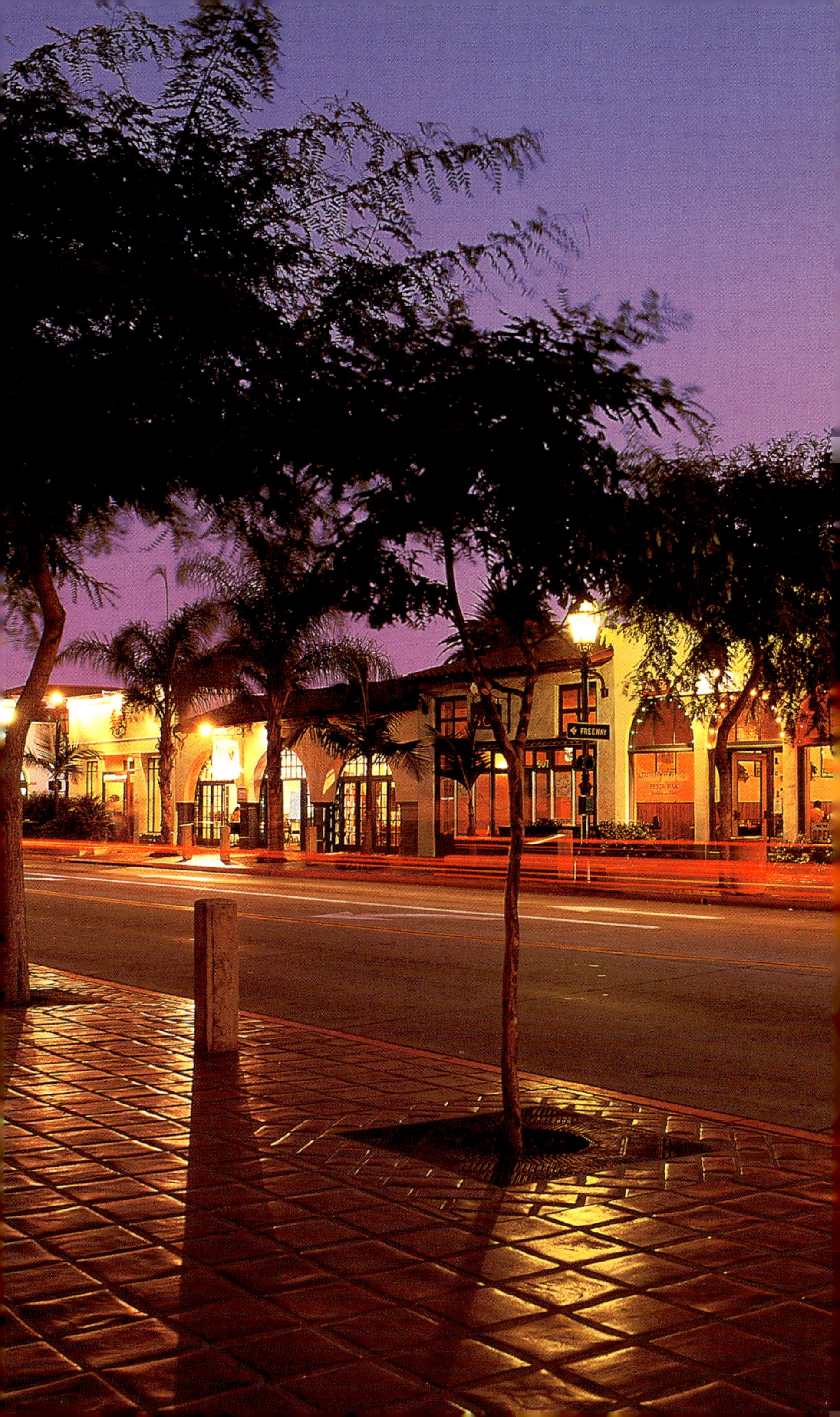
FREEWAY
RESTAURANT

692
830
Hobie
00237
2747
7761
TACKLE SHACK
WATERSPORTS
800-537-6099

Public Transportation
Metropolitan Transit District, 683-3702

Entertainment Info
The Independent free newspaper, published Thursdays, available at news racks, restaurants, hotels, www.Independent.com
The Santa Barbara News-Press daily newspaper publishes a calendar, www.news-press.com

Upcoming Performing Arts Events
Santa Barbara Performing Arts League free, bi-monthly performance guide, 563-8068, or www.sbperformingartsleague.org

A Solitary Beach Walk
East Beach to **Butterfly Beach** near the Biltmore

Golf
Sandpiper Golf Course, 7925 Hollister Ave., 968-1541

Book Hotel Reservations On-Line (or Ask for a Free Visitor's Guide to Be Mailed)
www.santabarbaraCA.com, (800) 676-1266, or (805) 966-9222.

Picnic Spot
Orpet Park, Alameda Padre Serra and Moreno Road
Chase Palm Park by the Chromatic Gate, along E. Cabrillo Blvd.

Picnic Supplies
See chapter 2

A Lavish Brunch with a View
Biltmore Hotel, 1260 Channel Drive, Montecito

A Parking Place
City lots are located on either side of State St. at the Amtrak Station (209 State St.), along the beach, and at the Visitor Center, at E. Cabrillo Blvd. and Garden St.

Rent a Bike or In-Line Skates
Wheel Fun Rentals, 22 State St., 966-6733

Birding
Botanic Garden
Andree Clark Bird Refuge
The **sand spit** at the breakwater

Solitude with a View
Hilda McIntyre Ray Neighborhood Park, 1420 Kenwood Rd.
Also see chapter 4

Help with Last-Minute Accommodations (during the Week)
The Visitor Center, in the kiosk at 1 Garden Street across from the beach

Bar with Appetizers and Cheap Drinks at Happy Hour
(note: Thursday night is college night)
El Paseo, 10 El Paseo
SoHo Restaurant and Music Club, 1221 State St.
The Wildcat, 15 W. Ortega St.
Sharkeez, 416 State St.

Catamarans Near the Harbor

SEE A 72-FOOT BLUE WHALE SKELETON
Santa Barbara Museum of Natural History (also has Chumash basketry and other exhibits), 2559 Puesta Del Sol Road, 10 A.M. to 5 P.M. daily, 682-4711.

MEET A LOCAL ARTIST
Sunday Arts and Crafts Show at the Beach, Cabrillo Blvd.

UPSCALE SHOPPING
Paseo Nuevo, in Santa Barbara.
Coast Village Road, in Montecito

LOW-END SHOPPING
Alpha Thrift, 1123 State St.

WINE TASTING
Wine Cask / Intermezzo, 813 Anacapa St.
East Beach Wine, 201 South Milpas St.
Santa Barbara Winery (also offers guided wine tours), 202 Anacapa St., 963-3633

DANCE CLUBS
Mostly in the lower State St. area

TAKE A TRAIN RIDE AMONG THE ANIMALS
Santa Barbara Zoological Gardens, 500 Ninos Drive, 10 A.M. to 5 P.M. daily. A 30-acre park with more than 600 animals in naturalistic habitats.

INEXPENSIVE MEXICAN FOOD DOWNTOWN
Los Arroyos, 14 W. Figueroa St.

Chilangos, 503 State St.

WINE WITH A VIEW
Encanto Hotel on the Riviera, 1900 Lasuen Drive
Brown Pelican Restaurant at the beach, 2981 Cliff Dr.

A ROCK CONCERT
Santa Barbara Bowl, 1122 N. Milpas St., call 962-7411 for information

WATCHING YACHT RACING
Wednesday afternoons in the summer, from Shoreline Park or the edge of the breakwater

WATCHING HANG GLIDERS
Gibraltar Rd.
Douglas Family Preserve

FISHING
West Beach
The pier, west of the Wharf

A WAY TO SEE THE TOWN IN 90 MINUTES
Old Town Trolley Tours, 965-0353 *(you can get off and board again, for a more leisurely trip)*

GREAT THAI RESTAURANT WITH TAKE-OUT FOOD
Zen Yai, 425 State St., 957-1102.

NOT DOWNTOWN BUT WORTH THE TRIP
Chaucer's Books, largest independent bookstore in California, 3321 State St.

Vices and Spices: neighborhood coffee shop, 3558 State St.
Lake Cachuma, a Santa Barbara County Park with nature cruises, camping, great fishing, 18 miles outside of Santa Barbara on Highway 154, 686-5054.

Coldspring Tavern, stagecoach stop with food and cowboy music, at the top of San Marcos Pass on Highway 154, on the way to Lake Cachuma, 967-0066.

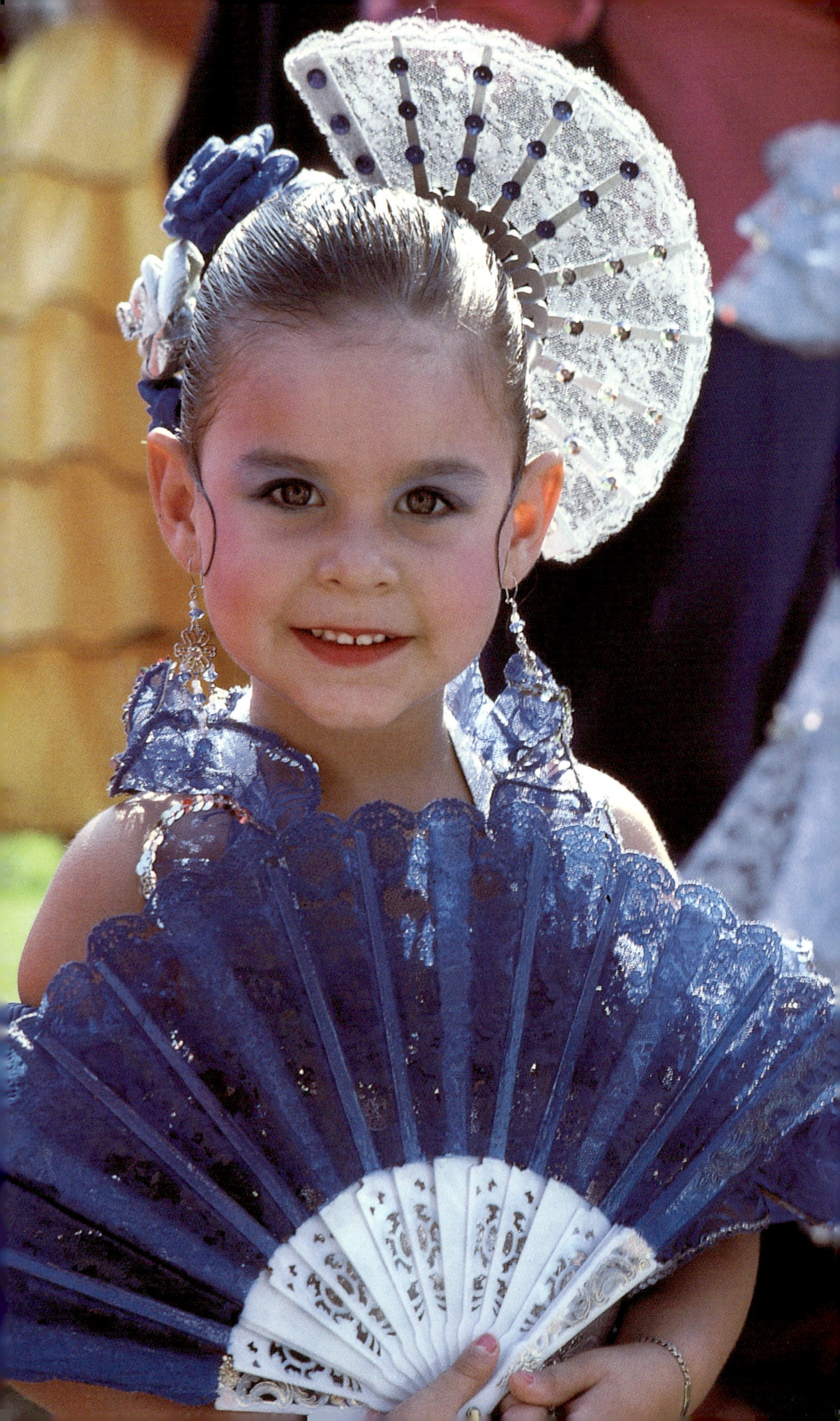

Celebrations and Seasonal Events

Due to the changeable nature of the dates and locations of the events listed here, for up-to-date information, either call the listed number (area code 805); check a local publication, such as the Santa Barbara Independent newspaper, www.Independent.com; or call the Santa Barbara Chamber of Commerce, 965-3023.

January
Whale Watching - California gray whales migrate through our waters January through April (see chapter 2). 897-3187.
Hang Gliding Festival - 965-3733.
Eagle cruises at Lake Cachuma - November through February, take a two-hour guided cruise to watch eagles soar. 686-5054.

February
International Film Festival - A week-long screening of the new U.S. and foreign films, including tributes to, and lectures by Hollywood stars and screenwriters. 963-0023.
Whale Festival - Local marine mammal exhibits, classic car show, arts and crafts, and live entertainment celebrate the gray whale migration. 966-0500.

March
Santa Barbara International Orchid Show - Growers and buyers from around the world converge to enjoy a dazzling display of orchids. 967-6331.
Kite Festival - Kite lovers share their passion at this more-than-15-year-old event. 967-4511, ext. 106.

April
Presidio Days - Three-day event celebrating Santa Barbara's birthday at the historic Presidio. 966-9719.
Santa Barbara Fair and Expo - Traditional country fair at Earl Warren Showgrounds. 687-0766.
Earth Day - Appreciate and learn about the environment at a festive gathering on the grass. 963-0583.
Jewish Festival - Celebration of Jewish arts, food, and culture. 963-0244.

May
Cinco de Mayo Festival - Mexican celebration with food, crafts, and mariachi music. 965-8581.

Children's Festival - Alameda Park benefit for the Family Service Agency, with fun for kids. 965-1001.
I Madonnari - Chalk street painting at the Old Mission on Memorial Day weekend, with food and music, free admission. 569-3873.
Irish Festival - Celebrate Ireland and her music, dance, food, and art. 687-4343.

JUNE
Summer Solstice Celebration - Local artists and wits take to State Street at noon in a parade celebrating the longest day of the year; entertainment follows through evening. 965-3396.
Big Dog Parade and Canine Festival - Dogs and their wacky owners woof it up.
Semana Nautica - Athletic competitions on land and in the water through the months of June and July. 965-0509.
Santa Ynez Live Oak Festival - Music at Lake Cachuma for the weekend or the day!
Volleyball Tournaments - At East Beach.
Writer's Conference - Successful authors provide personal knowledge of the literary world for developing writers. 684-2250.
Caribbean Festival - Dance, music, food, and fun with abandon!
Music Academy Summer Festival - Symphony and chamber music concerts, opera, master classes, and picnic concerts, through August. 969-4726.
Chinese Festival - Food, culture, and art from China. 964-0038.
Oak Group Art Shows - Display and sale by a large local group of environmentally conscious artists. 962-9111.

JULY - INDEPENDENCE DAY
Santa Barbara Symphony - Free concert on the grass at the Courthouse Sunken Garden.
Art Festival at the Mission - With music and dancing. 564-0199.
Stow House Old Fashioned 4th - Goleta hosts the all-American fun day at a historic location.

JULY - OTHER EVENTS
Santa Barbara National Horse and Flower Show - One of the top U.S. equestrian events, in conjunction with a flower show, at Earl Warren Showgrounds. 687-0766.
Santa Barbara Orchid Fair - 50 guest orchid vendors, at the Horse and Flower Show. 967-1284.

French Festival - Eau la-la! The food! The culture! The entertainment! 564-PARIS.
Greek Festival - Celebrating Greek culture with food, music, and art. 683-4492.

August
Fiesta - Santa Barbara's oldest celebration of our Spanish/Mexican past, including five days of parades, music, food, and dancing in several locations throughout the city. 962-8101.
Wine Festival Weekend - Weekend at the Natural History Museum, presenting a celebration of food and wine. 683-4711.
Festa Italiana - Be Italian for the weekend! Food, entertainment, and art. 565-2968.

September
Concourse d'Elegance - Beautiful old classic cars on exhibit
Jazz Festival - All-star lineup performs on the sand at the beach. 800-480-3378.
Organic Festival - Booths, drawings, demonstrations, instructions and give-aways in Oak Park.
Renaissance Faire - Campgrounds near Lake Cachuma is transformed into 16th-century England. 682-0310.
Multicultural Festival - Celebrate diversity! 564-4343.
CALM Antique Show - Antiques and decorative arts at Earl Warren Showgrounds. 898-9715.

October
Art Walk at the Natural History Museum - Over 100 artists and artisans from all over the West display their art along beautiful Mission Creek. 682-4711.
Fiddler's Convention - Live music and contest outdoors. 964-4407.
Lemon Festival - Goleta hosts the celebration of everything lemon with crafts and entertainment. 967-4618.
Avocado Festival - Carpinteria hosts the guacamole lover's dream with crafts and fun. 684-0038.
Fiesta City Cat Show - Competition among the cats-certain to be the season's meow. 687-0766.

November
Day of the Dead - All Saint's Day as celebrated in Mexico.
National Amateur Horse Show - West Coast training show, English and Western divisions. 687-0766.

December
Messiah Community Sing-Along - Everyone's invited to join the chorus at a lovely local church. 966-4131.
Day of Our Lady of Guadalupe - Catholic Saint's Day especially remembered in the Mexican community.
Santa Barbara Downtown Holiday Parade - All the lighted floats and the big guy in red make their State Street appearance. 962-2098.
Harbor Festival of Lights - Local marine celebration floats a parade of watercraft decorated with holiday lights from East Beach to the Harbor. 564-5531.

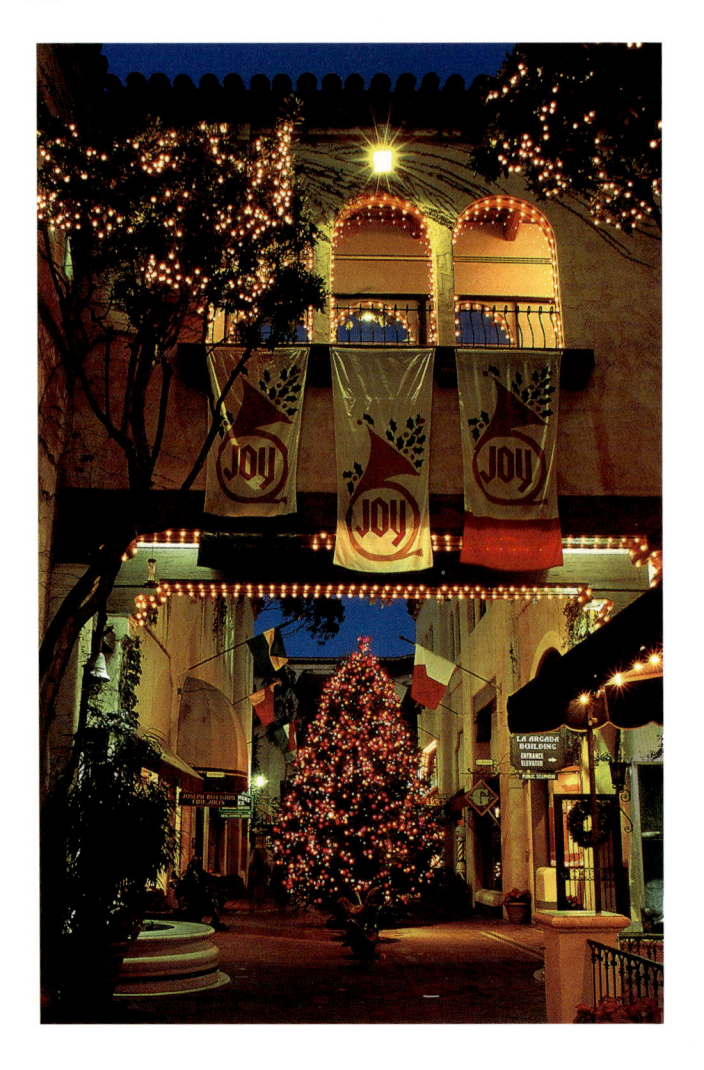